# BOTANY FOR DESIGNERS

# BOTANY FOR DESIGNERS

## A PRACTICAL GUIDE FOR LANDSCAPE ARCHITECTS AND OTHER PROFESSIONALS

### KIMBERLY DUFFY TURNER

EDITED BY RONDA M. BRANDS

W. W. NORTON & COMPANY

NEW YORK · LONDON

For information about permission to reproduce selections from this book,
write to Permissions, W. W. Norton & Company, Inc., 500 Fifth Avenue, New York, NY 10110

For information about special discounts for bulk purchases, please contact
W. W. Norton Special Sales at specialsales@wwnorton.com or 800-233-4830.

Composition and book design by Jonathan D. Lippincott
Manufacturing by 1010 Printing International Limited
Production Manager: Leeann Graham
Digital production: Joe Lops

Library of Congress Cataloging-in-Publication Data
Turner, Kimberly Duffy.
   Botany for designers: a practical guide for landscape architects and other
   professionals / Kimberly Duffy Turner; edited by Ronda M. Brands. — 1st ed.
      p.   cm.
   Includes bibliographical references and index.
   ISBN 978-0-393-70624-6 (hardcover)
   1. Planting design. I. Brands, Ronda M. II. Title.
SB472.45.T87 2011
712'.2—dc22
2010034200

ISBN 13: 978-0-393-70624-6

W. W. Norton & Company, Inc., 500 Fifth Avenue, New York, N.Y. 10110
www.wwnorton.com
W. W. Norton & Company Ltd., Castle House, 75/76 Wells St., London W1T 3QT
0 9 8 7 6 5 4 3 2 1

# CONTENTS

# ACKNOWLEDGMENTS

I wish to acknowledge with gratitude everyone who helped contribute to this manuscript. This book would not have been possible without the dedication of my publisher, W. W. Norton & Company, and my editors, Andrea Costella Dawson and Ronda Brands. Thank you for your many hours of editing, your organizational input, and for all of the probative questions that helped to strengthen this work.

Thank you to my former students and colleagues at the Boston Architectural College for helping me to hone the curriculum for the course, which served as the starting point—and title—of this book. To all my colleagues who contributed images, knowledge, opinions, and support, including Colin Brice and Caleb Mulvena of Studio Mapos; Derrick Choi of XChange Architects; Christopher Chapin; Tim Sheehan; Laura Knosp; James Freeborn of Select Horticulture; Lizza Smith of Cavicchio Greenhouses; Bill Mitchell; Ray Dunetz; and my former colleagues at Ryan Associates, thank you for your assistance and guidance. In particular, I'd like to thank Marcus Gleysteen and his team at Gleysteen Design, including Chandon Georgian, for your help in supplying some wonderful imagery and architectural insights. I'd also like to extend a special thank you to Garland Farm, Dennis Bracale, and the owners and gardener of Kenarden in Bar Harbor, Maine for allowing me to visit and photograph their properties and for offering their knowledge and insight.

Thank you to my friends and family, especially my mother, who have offered their unwavering moral support and psychic relief throughout this process and beyond. A special thank you to my brother, Adam Turner, for all your time and support, and for producing so many lovely images for this publication. This book is dedicated to my son, Lucas, and my partner, Ken, to whom I owe more than the lines on this page can reflect.

# BOTANY FOR DESIGNERS

# INTRODUCTION

In 2006, I began teaching a course at the Boston Architectural College titled Botany for Designers. It was meant to fulfill a science credit for the students and teach them the basics of botany. When registration for the course opened, I fully expected most, if not all, of the students to be landscape architecture majors; however, when the final roster was produced in the days preceding the first class, I was surprised to find that a good majority of my students were, in fact, architecture majors, with a few interior design majors. Most of these students were excited to learn how they could improve their abilities in creating sustainable designs. Knowing full well that designers are visual people, with a vocabulary that is weighted more towards space and art, I faced the challenge of how I might present this material, which is so scientifically based, in a way that would be best received by my students.

There was no doubt in my mind about the importance of this topic. Having received my undergraduate degree in horticulture—taking course after course in botany, plant pathology, soil science, and greenhouse and nursery management—I had a solid understanding of how botany can inform design. But when I was studying for my master's in landscape architecture, I was perplexed as to why the curriculum included only one or two courses on plants. Landscape architects must be well versed in grading, drainage, structural engineering, materials and construction, spatial relationships, pedestrian and vehicular circulation, and so forth, but we are also planting designers; surely the topic warrants more than one or two courses, especially when the sustainability and ecological aspects of our jobs are so integrally related to plants. Although plants are among our most important tools for effective design, a surprisingly large number of landscape architecture curriculums across the country lack any horticulture or botany classes. These topics are nonexistent in architecture curriculums, yet many architects provide landscape design as part of their services. Even programs in garden design are often lacking in botany coursework, emphasizing instead design and plant identification.

This book is meant to be a primer to help fill that gap. A search for a comprehensive textbook for my course turned up nothing, so I spent hours piecing together readings from botany texts, planting design texts, and architectural journals, asking friends and colleagues to contribute any articles or bits of information they had. My course notes came to fill a six-inch thick three-ring binder, the contents of which I have adapted to share here in the hope that a topic or two will expand your knowledge base and offer a new perspective on plants and design.

## PRACTICAL APPLICATIONS OF BOTANY

Plants are a critical part of our world, providing us with food and a habitable environment as well as sensory enjoyment (Fig. IN-1). As designers, we use plants in a variety of ways, as both functional and aesthetic components of our designs, yet few of us have had the opportunity to study plants in depth, to delve into the botany or science of plant life in order to understand their basic needs for survival and the reasons why plants look and

function the way they do. Architects, landscape architects, garden designers, and other design professionals can benefit from considering the basics of botany, and this knowledge can assist us in selecting the appropriate plant material and expanding our plant palette, provide us with a language with which to discuss our designs with one another and others across other disciplines, lend inspiration to our designs, and help us influence environmental and ecological integrity.

### PLANT MATERIAL SELECTION

Designers who specify plants should know the basics of good plant material selection, choosing plants well suited not only to the design but also to the environmental conditions of the site. Likewise, designers should also be able to select healthy plant material in the nursery and to identify and reject compromised materials when they arrive at the job site.

Every designer's goal is to have his or her designs withstand the test of time. For landscape architects and garden designers, a substantial measure of achieving that goal is whether our plant selections mature in a way that continues to enhance our design intent—whether it is to create an intimate space, direct a view to a distant vista, or focus attention toward a place of congregation or interest. For architects, the goal may be to enhance a particular architectural feature or unify building and landscape. To achieve lasting results, we must understand the living elements of our designs— plants— and how

IN-1 An allée of katsura trees in autumn. These trees emit a sweet fragrance like cotton candy as their leaves change color.

they interact with their environment. We will then be able to link our plant choices more effectively to the variable existing conditions of the job site and continually expand our plant palette to widen our choices. This book will serve as a fundamental resource to allow designers to tackle these goals successfully.

## A CROSS-DISCIPLINARY LANGUAGE

Botany is presented here in accessible terms in order to provide designers with a vocabulary that will enhance our practice and help us communicate more successfully with one another. This vocabulary will also help us effectively communicate with practitioners of related disciplines, such as contractors, maintenance crews, nursery employees, lumberyard staff, arborists, and conservation commission administrators, among others.

## INSPIRATION FOR DESIGN

Plants have influenced the design of the built environment throughout human history. The natural forms of plants are not only beautiful but almost always functional as well. Examples of this mimicking of nature in architecture are abundant—from the fluted columns of Egyptian tombs to the cantilevered forms of contemporary architecture—as are examples of the forms, patterns, and proportions in nature informing landscape and garden design.

## ENVIRONMENTAL AND ECOLOGICAL INTEGRITY

Every day, we make decisions that influence the environment around us. We choose whether or not to use organic products, cultivate our own gardens, recycle our waste, conserve energy, or become active in environmental groups. As designers, we have an even more profound influence on environmental and ecological integrity. We have the opportunity to reclaim and remediate wetlands, protect sensitive sites, cultivate urban wilds, create sustainable landscapes and "green" developments, and influence and educate our clients and our communities. A basic understanding of botany can help us evaluate new trends and technologies in "green design" and make decisions that promote sustainability.

## AN OVERVIEW

By providing a broad overview of botany, this book is meant to be a starting point to encourage designers to explore the world of plants in a new way, to arm us with the tools to ask the right questions, and to inspire us to

educate ourselves continually on the importance of plants.

The chapters cover a variety of topics in plant science, with detailed explanations and examples of how these topics relate to design. This approach is meant to provide direct links between botany and design and quick references to assist you in applying these discussions to your daily practice.

The appendices provide handy references for common botanical terms used in horticulture, plant lists for various plant features and requirements, and suggestions for further reading.

The first chapter, "What's in a Name?" explains the fundamentals of the plant lexicon and how plant systematics, nomenclature, and classification can provide us with clues about a plant's appearance, origin, usefulness, and characteristics.

Chapter 2, "The Science of Cells: Keys to Plants' Cultural Requirements," provides a description of plants' most basic building blocks: cells. Plants' requirements for light, soil, water, and nutrients are explained, including how construction (structural) soils differ from forest (planting) soils. The particular challenges of urban conditions are explored, with tips on selecting plants and situating design elements for city environments.

Design is perhaps most informed by our perceptions of a plant's spatial and visual characteristics, which are based on the plant's morphology (its physical form and external structure), the subject of Chapter 3. Various aspects of plants (habit, leaves, bark, flower, fruit, etc.) can serve as design features. Because color is such an important part of our perceived environment, the following chapter, "Color in Planting Design," addresses this expansive topic with a basic overview of color theory and a discussion of how to utilize plant colors (from leaf, flower, bark, etc.) to enhance design.

A plant's morphology also provides insight into its potential functional use in design, the subject of Chapter 5. As spatial elements in the landscape, plants can integrate architecture and landscape; encourage or prohibit physical and visual access; enhance architectural features; visually manipulate the sense of space; and promote environmental comfort and safety.

Chapter 6, "Cues from Nature: Plants as Design Inspiration," explores the various ways in which designers can mimic the natural forms, patterns, and proportions found in the plant world to create functional and aesthetically pleasing spaces. Beyond the interplay between symmetry and asymmetry, this chapter considers the naturally occurring space and scale ratios that are prevalent in plant life and that can also be mimicked to create spaces for human comfort, peace, and tranquility.

Realizing our design visions in the landscape requires us, as designers, to gain expertise in numerous skills involved in design installation but based in botany, and these are covered in Chapter 7. We need to be adept at specifying plant material and examining and selecting plants in the nursery, knowing what to look for in terms of good structure and health. On the job site, our informed super-vision of planting, transplanting, and pruning will help ensure the long-term success of our projects. Providing landscape care-givers and maintenance crews with effective and comprehensive maintenance plans is yet another element in the long-term success of our designed landscapes. Because roots present their own unique challenges in the landscape, one section of this chapter explores what designers need to know in order to prevent or resolve problems like pavement and utility damage and to create environments that allow roots to coexist with other features of the built environment.

The following chapter, "Manipulating Plant Forms," covers basic pruning techniques as well as more extreme forms of physical manipulation, such as coppicing, pollarding, pleaching, topiary, espalier, layering, and grafting. Chapter 9, "Choosing Wood for Hardscape," explores how the differing characteristics of the available types of wood lend themselves to various interior and exterior applications.

The final chapter, "Nature's Solutions: Green Design Strategies," discusses the growth of the "green" movement, the trend of LEED standards, and the rationale for sustainability as an important concept for design professionals, focusing on key sustainable practices related to botany. Topics include environmental benefits of plants (including the use of green roofs and vertical gardens), sensitive materials selection, and biomimicry, the concept of taking inspiration from nature to solve design problems in sustainable ways. A discussion of how coevolution, symbiosis, and botanical adaptations can be utilized in design leads to a brief description of plant evolution. We as designers can use lessons in nature to inform the evolution of our own useful and adaptive designs in both building and landscape architecture.

It is my hope that this book will be used as a resource and a reference for designers, offering basic instruction in botany and tips on how to use this information to advance our designs and promote the health and success of our environments.

# 1

## WHAT'S IN A NAME?

Designers are faced every day with the challenge of effectively communicating our ideas. As visual people, we generally feel most comfortable communicating with images and sketches, but we also utilize our own "design lingo," referring to *space, program, movement*, and *form*. These terms can mean very different things to us than they do to someone in another profession, such as an aerospace engineer, a musician, or an athlete; these variations in definitions are distinct and important and often make the difference between effective communication and exchanges that leave both parties confused. Conversely, understanding the precision of terminology can enrich conversations across disciplines.

The language of botany is one that can truly assist designers in elevating our work. An understanding of plant classification and nomenclature can benefit us in selecting the proper plant and communicating with our clients, with professionals in the "green" industry, and with one another. While the chapters that follow explore the internal and external characteristics of plants, this chapter examines how the names and classification of plants can inform our work as designers. There are currently thought to be approximately 350,000 species of plants on earth, but our emphasis is on the much smaller group of trees, shrubs, vines, perennials, and annuals most often used as ornamentals in design.

## THE LEXICON

Every science has its own unique lexicon. The systematics (method of classifying and organizing) and nomenclature (naming) of plants have much to say about plant characteristics (that is, design features) and often reveal information about a plant's appearance, origin, or usefulness. The system of scientific, or botanical, names used today has its roots in a method created in 1753 by Carolus Linnaeus, a naturalist and professor of medicine and botany in Stockholm, Sweden. Linnaeus utilized a two-word, or binomial, system—a shorthand of sorts—consisting of a generic (genus) name and a species epithet. For ease of pronunciation and memory, people have given nearly every biological organism a common name as well; these names vary by region and country and so are not uniquely paired to each organism, as are botanical names.

## GENUS AND SPECIES

In today's binomial nomenclature, the genus is a noun, which is always capitalized, and the species epithet is an adjective, which is written in lower case. The species name is a combination of the two. The entire name is either underlined or italicized (*Acer rubrum*, for example). Because these names are intended to be used by people in any country, speaking any language, they are generally created in Latin (or sometimes a "Latinized" version of a word or name), a language that is no longer spoken by native speakers as their main language and, thus is no longer changing. In this way, speakers of any language can properly identify and communicate about any one species of plant without a language barrier.

Since the species epithet is descriptive, a basic understanding of botanical Latin terms (and Greek terms, which are also often used) can sometimes help us determine a plant's

1.1 *Acer rubrum* gets its species epithet from its scarlet fall color.

important characteristics, origin, or usefulness. For example, one form of the Latin word for *red* is *rubra*. Therefore, plant species with striking red coloration are often given the species name *rubra*, or a variation on the term. Again, using the earlier example of *Acer rubrum* or red maple, we may wonder why this particular species of maple, which has green leaves in spring and summer, would be given such a name (Fig. 1.1). Those familiar with this species will know that the fall foliage color of this maple is crimson, as are its leaf petioles and its marginally showy flowers.

Knowledge of these terms is a handy tool for designers to use when selecting plant material for the landscape. See Appendix A for a list of common botanical Latin and Greek terms.

## COMMON NAMES

Because botanical names tend to be difficult to pronounce, understand, remember, and spell, many plants have also acquired regionalized, vernacular names for general use. For example, a common name for *Betula papyrifera* is paper birch, a name much easier to learn than its scientific equivalent. Common names are usually written in lowercase and are neither underlined nor italicized.

These common names are sometimes translations of their scientific counterparts, but they often vary greatly, not only from language to language but also from region to region. Where confusion begins to set in is when there are many different common names for the same plant. For example, *Arctostaphylos uva-ursi* is a groundcover with a fairly wide distribution and a long history of medicinal use. It has been given many common names in English, such as bearberry, kinnikinick, mealberry, hog cranberry, sandberry, mountain box, and bear's grape. Different common names may be used depending on region or personal preference, but all refer to this particular species of *Arctostaphylos*.

To further compound the problem, sometimes the same common name is used for many different species of plants. For example, bluebell is the common name for certain species of *Campanula*, *Hyacinthoides*, and *Mertensia*, all of which can be found in the United States, as well as *Sollya*, which is found in Australia. It is important for designers not to rely solely on common names when communicating plant selection choices unless we are certain the common name used is referring to the species of our choice. Also, it is imperative when communicating with clients to be sure that the plant they are requesting is, indeed, the plant you understand it to be. I once had a client ask for a "snowbell," and while I first assumed she was requesting a cultivar of *Viburnum*, she was, in fact, asking for a type of *Syringa* (lilac). Because I had brought photographs to our meeting, we were able to determine the correct plant.

## PLANT CLASSIFICATIONS

Modern plant classification groups categorize plants by biological type, based on Linnaeus's groupings but revised over the years to better align with Darwinian principles of evolution. Plants are classified and organized into various rankings or levels, each with increased specificity. This system gives each plant a unique place in the biological world that helps identify the plant and its relationships to other plants. In the most commonly used system, related genera are gathered into families, which share many biological features that are generally visually recognizable; related families are gathered into orders, and then classes, divisions (or phyla), and finally kingdoms (in this case, the plant kingdom).

In this book, we will focus on the six classifications most often encountered in the nursery and design industries: genus, species, subspecies, variety, hybrid, and cultivar.

- **Genus:** In the binomial system, the first word in a scientific name describes the genus, which is a group of related species of organisms.
- **Species:** The second word in a scientific name is the species epithet. A species (named by combining the genus and the species epithet) is a group of individual

organisms that are similar because they descend from a common ancestor and, although offspring may differ slightly, they generally share key common characteristics. They also do not generally interbreed, at least not freely in nature.

- **Subspecies**: When plants have wide distribution in the wild, evolution can work at different rates, especially within geographically isolated areas. Smaller groupings of plants can develop with slight but consistent (reproducible) variations from the original species. These genetically variant plants are considered subspecies and are denoted with the genus and species epithet followed by the abbreviation subsp. or ssp. and the subspecies name. An example is *Veronica spicata* subsp. *incana*, which varies from the original species *Veronica spicata* by having fuzzy, gray-green leaves that are more suited to arid grasslands.

- **Variety**: Similar to subspecies, but with characteristic botanical differences that tend to be less prominent, varieties are denoted with the genus and species epithet followed by the abbreviation var. and the variety name. Although the differences are not great from a genetic or botanical standpoint, from a design standpoint they are notable and often the reason for the selection. An example is *Salvia azurea* var. *grandiflora*, which varies from the original species by having showier flowers.

- **Hybrid**: Although species tend not to interbreed with other species in the wild,

1.2 *Magnolia x loebneri* is an example of a hybrid plant.

there are exceptions to the rule. When different species do interbreed, or when they are crossed intentionally in the laboratory, the offspring are termed hybrids. They are denoted with the genus name followed by an 'x' and then a new species epithet. An example is *Magnolia* x *loebneri*, which is a cross between *Magnolia kobus* and *Magnolia stellata*, bred by Max Lobner of Germany shortly before World War I (Fig. 1.2). (Very occasionally, genera are interbred; for example x *Mahoberberis*, a cross between the genera *Mahonia* and *Berberis*.)

- **Cultivar**: Cultivars are variants that do not occur in nature, but rather only in cultivation, in the nursery or botanical industry, through cloning or other vegetative reproduction. Cultivars are extremely important in the nursery and design industries because these specific variants have been produced for a particular feature, such as flower or leaf color, hardiness, fragrance, size, and so forth. Cultivars are denoted with the genus and species epithet followed by the cultivar name in single quotes and not italicized. An example is *Weigela florida* 'Wine and Roses', which was cultivated for its deep burgundy leaves and flowers (Fig. 1.3). Clearly, the extravagant name selected for this cultivar was meant to have some marketing value and attract the gardener or designer.

How does this information assist us in plant selection? Beyond the ability, already noted, to request and communicate our plant selection choices, a basic understanding of subspecies, varieties, hybrids, and cultivars often allows us to take our plant selection choices one step further. For example, when a client tells us that *Hydrangea* are among her favorite plants, but she doesn't like the fact that their bloom time is short, we can recommend the cultivar 'Endless Summer', which has a longer bloom time than the straight species (Fig. 1.4). There are also times when the straight species might be better suited than a cultivar; for example, in a native planting with the characteristics of a woodland or a prairie (Fig. 1.5). In this instance, plant characteristics that are more in keeping with the natural environment, with more subdued colors, natural growth habits, and potential wildlife habitat (some cultivars are created to reduce or eliminate fruit production) might be preferred.

1.3 *Weigela florida* 'Wine and Roses' is an example of a cultivar with a clever marketing name.

1.4 *Hydrangea* 'Endless Summer' is a cultivar that blooms longer than the straight species.

1.5 Straight species may be better choices for naturalistic plantings.

designing a public space and want to keep a particular plant bed low- growing in order to maintain a clear line of sight with less need for pruning, cultivars or varieties with dwarf characteristics might be good choices (Fig. 1.6).

We must also take into consideration availability. Often the straight species is less available in the nursery than a cultivar or variety. Or perhaps a cultivar you are very familiar with is no longer available, but a newer cultivar exhibits the characteristic you are looking for. Several years ago, I became very attached to a cultivar of *Geranium* called 'Johnson's Blue' after growing it in my own garden and marveling over the color and the repeat blooms. After a few seasons of specifying this cultivar, I was disappointed to discover that it was unavailable at my local wholesale nursery. Because I have a good working relationship with the nursery's buyer—she has gotten to know my plant preferences over ten years of working together—she suggested 'Rozanne' as a successful substitute. Nursery professionals often are very well versed in newer cultivars and varieties and can assist in locating the proper plant. It is important to note on your plant list why you are selecting a particular cultivar (flower color, height, resistance, etc.) so the nursery can help find a proper replacement if necessary. Many nurseries now publish regular newsletters or blogs that help design professionals stay up to date on the latest cul-

As designers, we should explore the special characteristics of cultivars, varieties, or hybrids that make them different from the straight species. Countless applications of this knowledge will arise in our design work. If a cultivar is more tolerant of a particular pathogen, then it may be a good choice, but if that pathogen is not a problem in your region, perhaps another choice is better. If you are

1.6 Dwarf varieties and cultivars are appropriate selections for public spaces where visibility is important.

tivars, varieties, and hybrids, so we may continue to expand and update our plant palettes. If a newsletter is not standard practice at your local nursery, a spring visit may be in order to check out the stock, speak with a professional about availability, and glean his or her observations and thoughts about particular selections.

## DEVELOPMENT OF PLANT VARIATIONS

Subspecies, varieties, hybrids, and cultivars are all examples of genetic modifications. These modifications occur either in nature,

with little or no intervention from humans, or in a laboratory by a scientist with a specific outcome in mind. An understanding of how plant variations occur or are created can help designers make informed, responsible choices from among the hundreds of new plants appearing on the market every year.

### GENETICS IN NATURE

Genetic information is contained within all the cells of every living organism on earth as DNA (deoxyribonucleic acid) molecules. It accounts for the similarities and differences among species and is passed on from generation to generation, sometimes as an exact copy but often with slight variations that are responsible for the wide range of characteristics among individuals. Long strands of DNA molecules are called chromosomes, and their sequence determines the specific traits of an organism. Sometimes changes can occur when DNA replicates. These changes are called mutations and can be either beneficial or detrimental to the organism. When mutations are detrimental, they cause disease, and when they are beneficial, they promote evolution of the species by creating a new characteristic that assists the individual in survival in some way. This new beneficial characteristic is then passed on to future generations.

Before scientists discovered DNA and the processes involved in genetics and heredity, it was thought that the traits from the parents of all species were simply blended together when they created an offspring. For example, it was believed that a parent plant with red flowers and a parent plant with white flowers would always produce offspring with pink flowers. If this were true, all members of any species would look alike within a few generations, and scientists soon started questioning the accuracy of this theory. Gregor Mendel, an Austrian scientist, is credited with first discovering the rules of genetics and inheritance in the 1860s. Mendel studied pea plants because of their fast-growing and easy fertilizing properties and discovered that the traits of the parents showed dominant and recessive characteristics that were passed down to their offspring. These characteristics were either expressed as an observable trait or not,

depending upon whether they were dominant or recessive. His theories were an enormous advancement in the understanding of genetics and the rules of inheritance.

At roughly the same time that Mendel was studying these rules, Charles Darwin was also making advancements in the study of genetics. Before Darwin, scientists believed that all species were created simultaneously in their present forms and had remained unchanged. Each species had an ideal form, and each individual was an approximation of that form. But with the development of geology and the discovery of fossils, important questions arose. That some plant and animal forms occurred in some layers of rock and not others and that certain plant and animal fossils closely resembled present- day plants and animals forced some natural scientists to question the old theories of genetics. Darwin visited South America and the Galapagos Islands and discovered in both locations organisms that were similar but with slight variations. For example, a similar cactus existed in both regions, but where a certain tortoise was present, the cactus had a stem, and where tortoises were absent, the cactus did not have a stem. Darwin concluded that the cactus had adapted to survive in the presence of a predator. Because all species have minor variations in their individual characteristics, the selection of some individuals and elimination of others is crucial to evolutionary change. Darwin theorized that individuals with favorable characteristics are more apt to survive and reproduce, thereby passing along their favorable, inheritable traits to their offspring, while other individuals with less favorable characteristics are more likely to die. Nature becomes the selective mechanism that defines what is "favorable" or "unfavorable," and the outcome is that the most adaptive individuals will survive.

## GENETICS IN DESIGN

In the 150 years since Mendel and Darwin provided their theories on genetics, scientists have continued to make great advancements in understanding how genetics and inheritance operate. Many of the most interesting variations in plant species have been discovered in nature and give us the interesting leaf variegations, vibrant colors, fragrances, and sometimes climate and disease tolerances that we use in our designs on a regular basis. As we have seen subspecies and varieties of plants are those that occur in nature, having botanical variations from their parent species that are not widely different from a genetic standpoint but provide recognizable and reproducible characteristics that are interesting in other ways. These differences often occur because of a slight genetic mutation or the representation of a recessive gene. On the other hand, cultivars are man-made modifications. These variants do not occur in nature, but can only be reproduced by cloning or other means of vegetative (asexual) reproduction. Cultivars are created for a specific feature such as color, fragrance, or disease tolerance, but rather than occurring naturally, they are created in a laboratory.

Because we now know how genetic information is transmitted within DNA, it is possible to remove individual genes from cells and splice them into the chromosomes of other plants. This process of gene manipulation, also known as genetic engineering, can produce plants with remarkable resistance to pathogens and insects, drought tolerance, salt tolerance, improved nutritional value, increased productivity, and so forth, and is being studied primarily in the agricultural world. There has been much debate in recent years as to whether or not genetic engineering is desirable, whether the benefits outweigh the risks, and whether it will have long-term impact on genetic diversity and nature's own unique ability to heal and adapt. While this book makes no judgment on the topic, it is mentioned here in the context of the design implications of both natural and man-made modifications.

The seemingly never-ending parade of plant varieties and cultivars arriving on the nursery market every year can make plant selection a daunting task. Many designers tend to hold tight to the handful of cultivars they have become comfortable with and avoid new introductions they are unfamiliar with. But instead of being confined to a few familiar faces, we can view these new introductions as palette- expanding. Perhaps we have avoided a certain species of tree, such as *Betula papyrifera*, because of its susceptibility to insects—in this case, bronze birch borer—but new cultivars, such as *Betula papyrifera* 'Whitespire' and *Betula nigra* 'Heritage', have become available that reduce or eliminate this susceptibility, allowing us new opportunities for design and diversity. Or perhaps a client is requesting a garden of one particular color, or of abundant fragrance, yet we want to use a variety of plants in the design. New cultivars and varieties may allow us to maintain some species diversity while indulging our client's preferences. For example, a garden of fragrant pink flowers may include *Hemerocallis* 'Rosy Returns', *Phlox paniculata* 'Eden's Crush', *Lavandula angustifolia* 'Jean Davis', *Daphne* x *burkwoodii*, and *Syringa* 'Miss Canada'. Perhaps the most exciting prospect for genetic advancement is the possibility of developing plants that can tolerate the harsh urban conditions and extreme climatic shifts we are currently experiencing.

Choosing from among this ever-increasing array of plant material, for an environment of ever-increasing extremes, can be further informed by our knowledge of plants' cultural requirements. The science of cells provides us with insights into a plant's basic functioning and needs.

# 2

## THE SCIENCE OF CELLS:
## KEYS TO PLANTS' CULTURAL REQUIREMENTS

What is a plant? When faced with this question, most people will recall their high school biology class and say that a plant is a living organism that is green and rooted in the earth. Some might add that plants are able to produce their own food and are uniquely able to clean our air. There are exceptions to every rule, however: some plants have leaves that are red or white, some float on the surface of the water, and others are parasitic and therefore do not produce their own food (Fig. 2.1). For our purposes, we will simplify the definition of a plant as a complex (multicellular), photosynthetic (able to produce its own food), nonlocomotive (rooted in the earth), living organism. In this chapter, we will explore the basic components of plants, how they operate and function, and how we can better understand plants' responses in order to adjust environmental conditions and help them to thrive.

2.1 Some plants, like this pond lily, float on the surface of water.

## CELLS: THE BUILDING BLOCKS OF PLANTS

Just as designers need to understand the building blocks of their designs— the components of the building, room, or garden— it is important for botanists to understand the

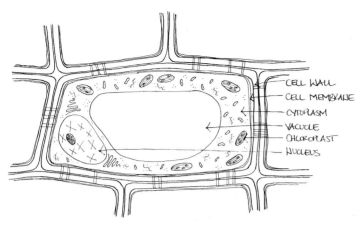

2.2 Plant cell.

components of cells are the cell wall, the cell membrane, cytoplasm, the nucleus, chloroplasts, and the vacuole (Fig. 2.2).

## CELL WALL

The cell wall is a tough yet flexible layer that surrounds the cell and contains a substance that is specific to plants called cellulose. Cellulose is a rigid material that protects the cell from attack by microbes, gives the plant physical strength, and prevents the bursting of cells during osmosis, which will be discussed below.

## CELL MEMBRANE

The cell membrane is a selectively permeable membrane that allows the passage of some materials and not others, and contains within it all the other components of a cell. This membrane allows the plant to protect itself against harmful toxins while still taking up important materials (such as nutrients and water). The uptake of water is possible through a process called osmosis, or the movement of water across the cell membrane according to the relative concentration of dissolved substances in the solutions on the inside and outside of the cell. For example, if you were to submerge a permeable balloon filled with a salt solution into a container of a saltier solution, the balloon would start to shrivel as water passed from inside to out-

building blocks of plants. From this knowledge, we can gain a greater understanding of how the overall plant structure operates and how it can remain healthy and functional. Cells form the basic structure of all life. Our bodies are comprised of cells, and so are the "bodies" of plants. The major difference between plant cells and animal cells is the presence in plant cells of chlorophyll and of a rigid material called cellulose in the cell walls. Chlorophyll is a green pigment that allows plants to engage in photosynthesis; cellulose allows plants to stand upright without "bones" and directs the passage of liquids, in a strawlike fashion, through the plant.

Plants are multicellular, or comprised of many cells. These cells are organized into types, and consistent types of cells having similar structure and function are called tissues. Tissues are further grouped together to form organs. The three major organs of plants are the stems, roots, and leaves, of which there will be much more discussion in later chapters.

At a very basic level, the six important

side through a process called diffusion (water passing from an area of higher concentration to one of lower concentration). In the case of the balloon, water passes to the outside of the balloon in order to equalize the salt solution both inside and outside the wall. If the salt were of a higher concentration inside the balloon wall, the water would pass from outside to inside, again in order to equalize the salt solution on either side of the balloon wall. If too much water diffuses into the balloon or cell, it will eventually burst from the pressure of the fluid. This, fortunately, is almost always prevented in plant cells by the rigid cellulose-containing cell wall.

If too much water diffuses *out* of the cell, however, it will shrivel, or dehydrate. For this reason, most plants do not thrive when exposed to too much salt— for example, road salt or high doses of fertilizers— as it can cause fatal dehydration. But, as we will see later in this chapter, some plants are more tolerant of salts, so in situations where we cannot change the nature of salt exposure, we can choose plants that might better tolerate this condition.

## CYTOPLASM

Inside the cell membrane is a watery substance called cytoplasm, in which all the other cell components are suspended. The cytoplasm is the site where most cellular activities occur.

## NUCLEUS

All plant cells, like animal cells, contain a nucleus. Within this nucleus is stored impor-tant genetic information (DNA) that determines all the qualities and functions of that cell. The nucleus is also considered the "control center" of the cell, as it controls all of its functions and responses.

## CHLOROPLASTS

Also contained within the cytoplasm, and unique to plants, are the chloroplasts. Chloroplasts contain a green-pigmented material called chlorophyll and are able to capture sunlight and transform it into energy through a process called photosynthesis.

## VACUOLE

Plants, having existed on earth for so long, have developed unique adaptations that assist them in survival. One of the most helpful adaptations is the development of a vacuole within the cell, a large sac that contains a majority of the stored water that a cell takes up. Even when a plant begins to lose water during drought, the vacuole works to maintain water pressure, or turgor pressure, to help control wilting. It is also uniquely able to take up excess mineral nutrients as well as toxic waste substances from the cell, and in this way help protect the plant from excesses of these materials.

## THE FUNCTION OF CELLS IN PLANTS

With an understanding of the basic components of cells, we can examine how they function and better comprehend how to support plant growth and survival and make responsible choices in both plant selection and maintenance.

## STRUCTURE

The rigid cell walls of plants contain a material called cellulose. Cells within a plant, depending on their function and genetic composition, form thicker or thinner cell walls. For example, the trunks of trees contain cells with very thick walls in order to help support the weight of the tree. A delicate leaf, on the other hand, needs only very thin cell walls, enough to prevent the rupture of the cell during water diffusion. In the example of the tree trunk, with increased age and size, cell walls may thicken by the addition of more cellulose, and also by the introduction of a hardening substance called lignin. Lignin makes wood stronger, denser, and more decay resistant, thus making certain types of lumber more valued than others for construction (see Chapter 9 for a detailed discussion of lumber in design).

## TRANSPORT

Within the stem of an herbaceous perennial, the branch of a shrub, and the trunk of a tree are two major tissue structures (groups of cells with similar functions and structures): xylem and phloem. These structures extend out into all the leaves and down to the roots of every plant and are responsible for the conduction of water and nutrients within the plant.

- **Xylem:** Primarily responsible for conducting water, some minerals, and certain organic compounds upward from roots to leaves, xylem is comprised mostly of dead cells. While xylem cells are found in all plants, a mature tree can be made up of as much as 70–90% dead xylem cells, which can translate into as much as 20% of the entire tree. A plant programs the death of these cells so they will become empty, lined end to end like a giant pipeline of millions of tiny straws to suck up water from the earth, through the roots, stem, and branches, and eventually into the leaves, by capillary action, a process called transpiration. Leaves of plants have tiny pores called stomata that open and close and allow microscopic droplets of water to evaporate. As these tiny droplets of water evaporate from the surface of the leaf, they attract new water molecules to take their place. Water, because of its unique bonding between atoms of hydrogen and oxygen, is an extremely "sticky" substance. The molecules are attracted to one another because of their unique cohesive bond, and in certain situations, such as in the giant redwoods, they can create columns of water that are hundreds of feet high.
- **Phloem:** Unlike xylem, phloem is comprised of living cells that conduct organic compounds, including nutrients and sugar produced during photosynthesis, primarily downward from leaves to roots. Whereas xylem only allows for flow in one direction (upward), the specialized

cells that comprise phloem also have the ability to transport this nutritive sugary solution, or sap, in multiple directions throughout the plant to areas that need it. Sap is generally transported in a downward direction to parts of the plant that are not photosynthetic, such as the roots, but it can also be transported from older to younger plant parts, including leaves that are not yet mature enough to produce their own food, flowers, fruits, and seeds, in order to support the growth of the plant. More information on the movement of nutrients within phloem will be found later in this chapter.

## THE ROLE OF PLANT HORMONES

Besides providing structure and transporting water, nutrients, and sugar, cells also contain substances that enable a plant to respond to its environment. They help ensure a plant's survival, and they reveal visual cues—such as wilting and yellowing—that can tell us that a particular environmental condition, such as lack of water or nutrients, is creating stress for the plant.

Much like humans, plants are continuously sensing and responding to external and internal signals, such as light, temperature, pressure, and gravity. These signals are received and transmitted to cell components that trigger a response in the plant. These signal molecules are called plant hormones, chemical compounds that are produced, in very small amounts, in one part of the plant and exert their effects on another part of the plant. Hormones are vital to plant growth and survival.

The five principal plant hormones are auxins, cytokinins, gibberellins, ethylene, and abscisic acid; additional hormones are being studied as research into cell functioning continues. Each hormone plays a specific role in plant growth and development, although many processes are a result of their acting in combination.

- **Auxins** are critical to fruit production and maturation as well as cell elongation and plant growth. They are responsible for the changes we see in plants when light, gravity, or other physical forces are altered, as well as when branches are pruned or damaged. Auxins are concentrated in the topmost (apical) buds of plant stems and suppress the growth of the lateral buds below them, a phenomenon called apical dominance. When an apical bud is removed, either by pruning or damage, the hormone concentrations shift to the next highest bud on the stem, triggering that bud to begin growing. Similarly, auxins also synthesize a response to light (phototropism), gravity (gravitropism), and touch (thigmotropism). Phototropism occurs when plant tips grow toward the light because auxins accumulate on the shady side of the plant and cause cell elongation. The differences in cell length on each side, with elongated cells on the shaded side of the plant, cause the branch to curve toward the light. Gravitropism allows plants, from the time they sprout from seed, to grow upward in response to the force of gravity. Thigmotropism is the reason why plants that mature in windy conditions tend to grow shorter and thicker, to withstand the force of the wind, and also why tendrils "know" to curl around a supporting structure.

- **Cytokinins** are plant hormones that have an anti-aging effect on plants. They are responsible for producing new shoots and adventitious roots, which are particularly important when plants need to increase sunlight capture or water and nutrient uptake from soils. Cytokinins are critical in rejuvenation pruning (see chapter 8), promoting a flush of new growth in older plantings that can revive an aging landscape.

- **Gibberellins** are responsible for stimulating cell division, promoting stem and leaf elongation, and causing seed germination. A lack of gibberellin causes a plant to become dwarfed, which may be a desirable quality if sufficient pruning maintenance is not feasible in a particular setting. An increase in gibberellin causes increased stem lengthening and flower and fruit size, which may be desired for aesthetic purposes.

- **Ethylene** is the plant hormone responsible for fruit ripening and leaf drop. Sudden leaf drop in a plant is an indicator of stress and warrants an inspection and potential alteration of environmental conditions. Ethylene is emitted in plants as a gas. Those in the cut flower industry know not to place cut flowers in an enclosed area with fruit. The ethylene gas emitted by the ripening fruit can cause the flowers to wither. By the same process, buds can be coaxed into opening by leaving them in close to a ripening piece of fruit.

- **Abscisic acid** helps plants cope with stress. It is responsible for slowing or stopping plant metabolism when growing conditions are poor and is also found in bud scales and seeds, where it acts as a growth inhibitor until conditions are more favorable for survival.

Our understanding of the role plant hormones play in growth can help us to predict how a plant will respond to our actions. We might prune a shrub or a tree, for example, to promote a flush of new growth. We can utilize site microclimatic conditions (wind, light, etc.) to shape plant forms: wind can cause stunted or irregular growth; shade can cause stems to elongate and leaves to grow larger than normal.

Synthetic plant hormones, sometimes called plant growth regulators, are commercially available, and they can help us further alter plant growth; some inhibit or retard growth in order to reduce the need for pruning or mowing, inhibit or promote fruiting or flowering to meet maintenance or aesthetic requirements, or stimulate root and shoot growth during propagation and transplant. From a design standpoint, the opportunities for altering plants' maintenance requirements and ensuring transplant success can be invaluable. However, there is some question about the long-term impact of certain growth regulators on the environment, as these regulators can include naturally-occurring hormones that have been artificially manipulated as well as chemicals not produced by plants, such as defoliants and herbicides. As always, we should be cautious about introducing these chemicals into our environments and ecosystems, especially when alternative plant selections are available.

## UNDERSTANDING PLANTS' CULTURAL REQUIREMENTS

Although it may be easy or commonplace to utilize plant material as just another object within a design, we have seen that not only are plants living organisms, but they also have a unique ability to adjust their functioning in order to respond to environmental conditions, and they often give us visual indicators that tell us whether they are thriving or struggling in their current conditions. Plants are by no means static objects in the landscape; they are constantly growing, changing, and interacting with their environment and other nearby organisms. In many ways, plants are more difficult to specify than any other element of a design because they must be considered both in the context of the environment in which they are being used and in time, not only by age but also by season. Environmental factors can cause extreme variations in growth. Sometimes these varia-

2.3 The windy microclimate along a riverbank has shaped this pine into an interesting sculptural form.

tions create pleasant anomalies, such as the sculptural form of a windswept tree (Fig. 2.3). At other times, these variations can cause us frustration because conditions outside our control (such as storms, pest introduction, and adjacent building developments that change light and drainage patterns) create inconsistencies that do not fit with the design, or worse, kill plants.

Because nearly every environmental condition a plant experiences triggers a response, a study of the site's microclimate is imperative for responsible plant selection. A close study of environmental conditions, such as local light levels, soils, and adjacent plantings, can make the difference between a successful planting and one that will not survive to maturity or capture the true intent of the design.

Human pressures, although difficult to predict, are also worth close study in order to ameliorate or prevent common problems such as vandalism and compaction by foot or vehicular traffic. Even with the most meticulous study of site conditions and an understanding of each plant's unique growth habit and life cycle, proactive landscape management and maintenance is still crucial in order to maintain the integrity of the design and assure that it will mature gracefully.

How do we select the appropriate plant materials for our designs? Understanding both plants' cultural requirements and job site conditions is the first step in selecting "the right plant for the right place." With the enormous diversity of plant species, cultivars, and varieties available on the market today, designers can often feel overwhelmed with decisions about plant choices. While the two-dimensional lines we draw on paper can fairly easily be translated into three-dimensional requirements in space, and individual plants can be selected with characteristics to meet design criteria, we must take the extra step in considering the basic cultural requirements of our plant selections. The following section outlines plants' basic cultural requirements, tolerances, and susceptibilities with regard to temperature, light, water, soil, air quality, and pests and diseases.

## TEMPERATURE

Plants use temperature as indicators. Most plants produce the most abundant growth when day and night temperatures are fairly comparable (approximately 10–15 degrees difference), such as in the spring. During these times, photosynthesis (the creation of sugars from sunlight) and respiration (the use of those sugars) are balanced. At very high temperatures, respiration greatly increases, while photosynthesis stays relatively constant, creating an imbalance in the production and use of energy and a slowing down of plant growth. At low temperatures, photosynthesis is greatly reduced and plants tend to enter into dormancy. Many plants require this period of rest in order to conduct other phases of their life cycle, such as flowering and fruiting. Different plants can withstand different variations in temperature based on their genetic predispositions. An understanding of the ranges of high and low temperatures that plants can tolerate is one important cultural requirement that will assist us in appropriate plant selection.

Hardiness zone is a geographically defined area in which a specific plant can survive based on the average minimum temperature of that zone or region. This classification system was first developed by the United States Department of Agriculture (USDA) in 1960 based on the previous ten to fifteen years of weather records. It was revised in 1990 (Fig. 2.4) and was due to be revised again in 2003, but the information has not yet been released. The map is divided into 11 zones with corresponding temperatures:

Zone 1: below -46°C (-50° F)
Zone 2: -46°C to -40°C (-50°F to -40°F)

Zone 3: -40°C to -34°C (-40°F to -30°F)

Zone 4: -34°C to -29°C (-30°F to -20°F)

Zone 5: -29°C to -23°C (-20°F to -10°F)

Zone 6: -23°C to -18°C (-10°F to 0°F)

Zone 7: -18°C to -12°C (0°F to 10°F)

Zone 8: -12°C to -7°C (10°F to 20°F)

Zone 9: -7°C to -1°C (20°F to 30°F)

Zone 10: -1°C to 4°C (30°F to 40°F)

Zone 11: above 4°C (above 40°F)

As a general rule, the lower zones are located at higher latitudes and elevations (temperate and tundra climates), while the higher zones are found at lower latitudes and elevations (tropical climates). A plant is considered to be "hardy to zone 6" if it can survive a minimum sustained temperature of -10°F, and it is assumed that the plant can withstand all the warmer zones as well. For example, a plant that is hardy to zone 6 should also be able to sustain temperatures in zones 7–11, although this is not always true. Some plants that are hardy to lower zones may not be able to survive sustained higher temperature extremes because of their genetic composition and their water and light requirements and may show signs of wilting, browning, and stunted growth that may eventually lead to plant death.

In response to this lack of reference to high temperatures, the American Horticul-

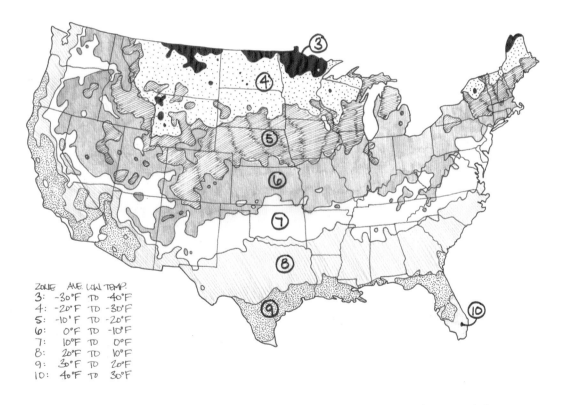

2.4 USDA hardiness zone map illustrating the zones of the continental U.S. (zones 1 and 2 are in Alaska; zone 11 is in Hawaii) (1990).

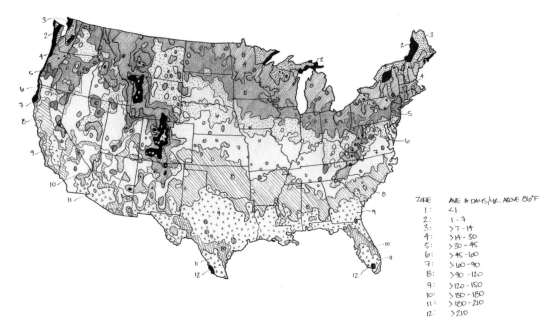

| ZONE | AVE # DAYS/YR ABOVE 86°F |
|------|--------------------------|
| 1: | <1 |
| 2: | 1-7 |
| 3: | >7-14 |
| 4: | >14-30 |
| 5: | >30-45 |
| 6: | >45-60 |
| 7: | >60-90 |
| 8: | >90-120 |
| 9: | >120-150 |
| 10: | >150-180 |
| 11: | >180-210 |
| 12: | >210 |

2.5  American Horticultural Society heat zone map (2003).

tural Society developed the heat zone map (Fig. 2.5). Regions within the same hardiness zone (i.e. with the same average winter low temperatures) can have very different summer temperatures. The heat zone map, much like the hardiness zone map, divides the United States into geographic areas (12 zones) that indicate the average number of days per year that zone experiences days over 86°F. More and more plants are now being coded not only for hardiness zone but also for heat zone, providing designers with more complete data when selecting plants.

Another factor not addressed by the USDA hardiness zones is reliability of snow cover. Changes in weather patterns, either annually or by climatic trend, make year-to-year snow cover extremely variable. Snow is

a natural insulator for plant roots and can protect plants from extremes in temperature. Actual temperatures below a layer of snow may be several degrees higher than the ambient temperature listed on the USDA hardiness zone map.

Other factors that can affect plants' tolerances to temperature include differences in soil moisture, humidity, wind, number of days of frost, and extreme fluctuations in temperature over short periods of time due to sun aspect and solar reflection. Therefore, while a good benchmark for plant selection, hardiness zones should be used as a guide, with site-specific (microclimate) conditions being taken into careful consideration. A microclimate is a localized region (from a few square feet to several square miles) where the climate (temperature, humidity, light levels, wind, etc.) differs from the surrounding area.

For example, a common issue in urban environments is sun and heat reflection from adjacent buildings. Plants, especially broadleaf evergreens such as *Rhododendron* sp. or *Ilex* x *meserveae*, are particularly sensitive to solar reflection, which can raise ambient temperatures several degrees very quickly during cold winter months. When these plants break dormancy too early in the spring or winter as a result of increased temperatures, they can suffer extreme desiccation as they try to take up water that is unavailable from the soil because it is frozen in the ground. Another common problem is winter trunk cracking (Fig. 2.6). Solar radiation in southern exposures can be quite strong, especially during winter months. The heat from the sun can cause the exposed southern side of a tree

trunk to break dormancy and take up water within its cells, and the water can then freeze, expand, and damage cells once temperatures again dip below freezing. The damage can be seen in the form of large, sometimes fatal, cracks in the trunk.

Alternately, microclimates can be used to our benefit. Southern exposures, enclosed, protected courtyard spaces, areas around bodies of water, and areas where wind and structures create a natural accumulation of snow cover are all places where microclimatic temperatures can be high enough to support the growth of more tender plantings, which might not otherwise survive in the local hardiness zone.

## LIGHT

Plants use pigment-containing molecules to sense light levels in their environments. These molecules, as well as hormones, are why seeds "know" not to germinate too deeply in the soil or under too dense a canopy, where energy stores are not available to allow the plant to survive until proper light levels are reached and it can begin photosynthesis. Likewise, flowering plants "know" to flower at a time when pollinators are available, because appropriate light levels an indicators of activity of those pollinators. Plants also "know" when to drop their leaves when winter is approaching because light levels and lengths are reduced.

Plants perceive two types of light: red/far-red and blue/UV. Molecules that perceive red and far- red light are called phytochromes;

2.6 Solar radiation in winter can cause bark in southern exposures to crack.

they control seed germination and the timing of flowering and dormancy, regulated by a phenomenon called photoperiodism, a plant's response to the length of light and dark in a day. Photoperiodism is extremely easy to manipulate. In the nursery industry, plants that usually bloom during longer days and shorter nights can be "tricked" into blooming during alternate times of the year by exposing them to artificial light in the middle of the night, the technique used to force poinsettias into bloom during the holiday season (Fig. 2.7).

Unfortunately, many plants are also tricked into blooming or delaying dormancy at less than ideal times by the presence of security, street, and landscape lighting, which can potentially cause damage to plants by altering their finely tuned seasonal cycles. As designers, we should avoid planting day-length sensitive plants, such as *Cornus florida*, *Betula papyrifera*, and *Rhododendron* sp., near these lights or provide baffles to deflect light from plants (Fig. 2.8).

Molecules that perceive blue and UV

2.8 Rhododendrons can be tricked into blooming at the wrong time of year by security lighting: this photo was taken in August.

light are cryptochromes, phototropins, and zeaxanthins. Cryptochromes help seedlings determine if there is enough light for photosynthesis or if they need to grow longer in order to reach an adequate light source. Phototropin allows plants to respond to changes in light direction, or track sunlight through the sky, as sunflowers do. Zeaxanthin plays a role in stomatal responses to light and protects plants from wilting.

As designers, we need to consider how much sunlight a plant requires in order to survive, and take care to specify plants that are suited to the light levels of the site. Plants have adapted over many years to grow in particular environments. In general, plants that are shade tolerant tend to have broader leaves in order to capture the small amounts of light

2.7 Poinsettias can be tricked into blooming in winter with light manipulation.

that penetrate the forest canopy, while plants that require more sun tend to have narrower leaves in order to protect them from too much water loss. Plants that are native to forest environments have very different light requirements than those native to prairie environments, and often cannot survive dramatic variations in light levels.

As a general rule, a plant that is said to require "full sun" usually requires six or more hours of direct sunlight in order to function properly (photosynthesize, bloom, fruit, etc.). A plant that requires "full shade" often cannot tolerate direct, sustained exposure to sunlight without suffering water loss or cellular damage. For these reasons, it is critical that designers understand the requirements of the plants we have selected. Likewise, it is also important to consider that as canopies mature, they will cast more shade on underlying plantings. Sometimes, adjustments in plant selection will need to be made as light levels evolve within a maturing planting design. See Appendix B for lists of plants that are shade tolerant and sun tolerant.

## WATER

Just as plants have adapted over many years to specific light environments, so too have they adapted to specific moisture conditions. As a general rule for a designed landscape, most plants require approximately 1" of water per week. However, it is important to note that this water should be applied in two to three applications (fewer, deeper waterings), as opposed to one or seven. Watering $\frac{1}{3}$" to $\frac{1}{2}$" two to three times per week encourages root systems to grow more deeply into the soil, which assists in soil structural stability and accessibility to nutrients. Watering too quickly and too often has the opposite effect, encouraging roots to grow more shallowly, which can make them susceptible to compaction and drought stress. A single watering per week of 1" or more is counterproductive because water will run off the soil surface as it becomes too saturated and will not be available to plant roots. There are, of course, plants that are more drought tolerant, adapted to more arid conditions; these will not require as much water, although other environmental conditions need to be conducive to their survival.

Designers must ensure that, where irrigation systems are not available, the proper plants are selected to match the natural precipitation levels of the environment. Where irrigation systems are installed, it is important, from a sustainability standpoint, to ensure proper functioning and maintenance of these systems and the selection of the best system for the site in order to conserve water. In evaluating options for irrigation, we can look to the many examples we have today of "closed systems" that redirect and reuse stormwater, including the design of topological depressions or "wells" or bioswales that collect rainwater and make it available to plants.

Often when plants are considered to be wetland tolerant, it is less an indication of their tolerance of copious amounts of water than of their tolerance of lower levels of oxygen in the soil. As we will see in the next section, water and air compete for the voids (or pore spaces) that exist between solids in the soil. Most plants require a balance of both water and air in order to function properly; however, some plants are adapted to wetland environments, where oxygen is less prevalent in the soil. Lists of both drought-tolerant and wetland-tolerant plants are included in Appendix B.

## SOIL

As much as 80% of all landscape problems begin below ground. Both the volume and composition of soils are critical to the health and function of plants as well as to the structural integrity of buildings, roadways, and other structures, though the requirements of each are very different. Herein lies the perpetual struggle that all designers confront: the interface between structural soils and planting soils.

Our built environment is full of roadways, buildings, walkways, and other structures that allow us to live, work, and travel from place to place. Often, we rely on plantings to soften the built environment and make it more habitable and aesthetically pleasing; for example, planting along the foundations of structures and along pavements. Because the soil requirements for each are so wildly opposing, the interface between them almost always presents a conflict, where one or the other requirement is not met. Because plantings are generally installed after structures and hardscapes, they are most often left

with the poorer soil condition, resulting in plants that struggle to survive in conditions where resources are sparse. Good garden soil is imperative to healthy plant growth. This section explains what constitutes good soil, where challenges lie, and ways to remedy common soil problems.

*Soil composition:* Soil consists of four major components: the inorganic or mineral portion, organic matter, water, and air. The relative volumes of these components determine whether soil is better suited to structures or vegetation. For example, a loamy soil, which is considered good for plant growth, is generally comprised of roughly 50% solids (45% mineral and 5% organic matter), 20–30% air, and 20–30% water, whereas a structural soil has a higher percentage of solids, almost none of which would be organic matter, and a lower percentage of air and water (Fig. 2.9). The air and water exist

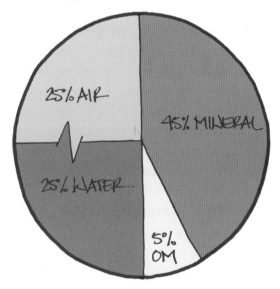

2.9 Appropriate composition of a loamy soil that supports plant growth.

within the voids of the soil, or its pore space. The mineral or inorganic components tend to make up a higher percentage of the volume of a soil and can be a source of both structural stability (for both plants and foundations) and nutrients necessary for plant growth.

The nutrients needed by plants include macronutrients (nitrogen [N], phosphorous [P], potassium [K], calcium [Ca], magnesium [Mg], and sulfur [S]) and micronutrients (chlorine [Cl], iron [Fe], boron [B], manganese [Mn], zinc [Zn], copper [Cu], molybdenum [Mo], and nickel [Ni]). Macronutrients are needed in higher quantities by plants than are micronutrients, which are generally only required in trace amounts. Most commercially available fertilizers contain nitrogen, potassium, and phosphorous because these are most often lacking in soils (or otherwise unavailable to plants because of pH or other factors), although each nutrient is important to plant growth and survival.

Plants often tell us if they are lacking a nutrient through various symptoms. For example, they display different patterns of chlorosis, or yellowing, based on deficiencies of nutrients. Chlorosis of older leaves is often an indicator of a lack of nitrogen, while chlorosis of younger leaves can be a sign of a calcium deficiency. Nitrogen and potassium are much more mobile nutrients than calcium, boron, and iron—that is, they are more easily transported within the phloem of a plant to the regions where they are needed during times of stress. This mobility may be compromised in older plants, causing the nitrogen deficiency and chlorosis; in younger plants a lack of calcium is often the culprit in chlorosis.

Yellowing can also occur between the veins of a plant (possibly indicating a deficiency of iron or manganese), as well as at the edges (suggesting a lack of magnesium or potassium). Unfortunately, other environmental conditions can skew or compound these symptoms. For example, poor drainage, soil compaction, and high pH can also lead to chlorosis, sometimes because these conditions prevent nutrient uptake, but also because they add additional stress to the plant. In these instances, simply adding nutrients to the soil will not resolve the problem; soil structure and/or drainage, discussed later in this chapter, must be remediated.

*Soil texture:* The mineral particles in soils are classified based on their particle sizes and include sand, silt, and clay. The proportions of these particles determine the texture of a soil and their arrangement determines the soil structure. Sand is generally between 0.05 and 2 mm in diameter and does not stick together but feels gritty to the touch. Silt is between 0.002 and 0.05 mm in diameter, is powdery when dry (it feels like flour or talcum powder) and somewhat sticky and moldable when wet. Clay is less than 0.002 mm in diameter, is highly moldable and sticky when wet, and combines into hard clumps when dry.

Clay is responsible for creating stable aggregates within soils. Because of its high surface area and surface charges, clay is important in exchanging ions in soil solution, which means it is responsible for making nutrients available to plants. Because of its small particle size, it can also hold and lose large amounts of water within its millions of tiny pores, which can cause it to swell and shrink, a phenomenon called expansive soil. This can be detrimental to structural foundations and plant roots. Therefore, too much clay can make soils conducive for neither planting nor structures. The maximum limit recommended for planting beds is 15% clay, and 27% is the maximum recommended for structural soils.

It is important to note that, depending on whether soils are being specified for structural or planting purposes, two different classification systems are used. The ASTM (American Society for Testing and Materials) classification system determines the standards for structural stability of soils and is used by architects and engineers in specifying soils and compaction levels that are suitable for foundations and structures. The USDA (United States Department of Agriculture) classification system, on the other hand, determines the suitability of soils for vegetation and is used by the forestry and horticultural industries, as well as landscape architects. Unfortunately, the particle size determinations for sand, silt, and clay are not the same for each entity's definition, so it is important to know which system is being used.

*Organic matter:* The organic matter portion of soil is the partially decomposed plant and animal material and other organic compounds produced by soil microbes. A very small percentage of organic matter has a large impact on plant growth, as it helps keep soil loose and friable and determines how much water and nutrients it can hold. Organic mat-

ter is imperative to healthy planting soil, as it is one of the most effective ways to improve soil fertility and structure and supports the growth of beneficial microorganisms, which in turn also improve nutrient and water uptake by plant roots. But organic matter also has detrimental effects on the stability of soils to support footings and foundations, as it tends to be spongy. A structural soil should have little to no organic matter.

*Pore space:* The water and air in soils are held within the voids between soil particles, or its pore space. Water not only holds nutrients in solution so they can be taken up by plants but is also fundamental to plant functioning. Very small pore spaces, such as those found between particles of clay, hold water much more tightly, since water is cohesive or sticky in nature, whereas large pore spaces, such as those between particles of sand, do not hold water very well. A sandy soil tends to be well drained. If there is ample water and the pore spaces are large enough to allow for its movement but small enough to hold it within the soil without allowing it to drain away too quickly, the water becomes available to plant roots. Air is also held within the larger pore spaces of soils, although it has a much different composition than atmospheric air. Soil air tends to be much more humid and has a higher concentration of carbon dioxide and a lower concentration of oxygen than the air we breathe. This environment is beneficial to plant roots, which require oxygen to function properly and carry out certain metabolic processes such as respiration.

*Soil problems and modifications:* Urban

conditions and construction create several problems within soil environments that make them much less conducive to plant growth. In other words, as soils are modified to be structural to support foundations and pavements, they become less able to support plant growth. Forest or plant soils must provide water, oxygen, nutrients, stability, a nontoxic environment, and room to grow. In a healthy, "natural" environment, a majority of these are provided within the topsoil, or the upper 5–7" of dark to light brown soil, which contains the required nutrients and water as well as the majority of plant roots. Beneath the topsoil layer is the subsoil, which is lighter in color, low in organic matter and pore space, and provides drainage as well as structural support. Often during construction, the topsoil is stripped away or otherwise modified to provide only the structural support required for building foundations and pavement bases, the subsoil is further compacted, and the entire soil profile becomes unsuitable for plant life. Organic matter is stripped away and pore spaces are minimized or eliminated and they no longer hold water or air.

The chemical composition of urban soils is also often modified. The pH of urban soils tends to be increased by leachate from nearby mortar and concrete. Soil pH is determined by the amount of hydrogen ($H+$) and hydroxide ($OH-$) ions in soil solution, and it is important to plants because it determines the availability of nutrients. A pH of 7 is considered neutral, while a pH higher than 7 (containing more $OH-$ ions) is alkaline and lower than 7 (containing more $H+$ ions) is acidic.

Some plants require either a more acidic or a more alkaline environment to function most efficiently, although most plants cannot tolerate a pH that varies far from neutral. The standard range of tolerance is between 6.5 and 7.5; although more of our commonly used ornamental plants prefer a slightly acidic soil around 6.5.

Designers can analyze soil for pH using a soil test, an invaluable tool in evaluating the precise conditions of the site soil for pH as well as nutrient availability, organic matter content, water content, exchange capacity, and sometimes microbial activity. While soil testing kits can be purchased at local home stores and nurseries, they tend to be far less sophisticated, often only testing for pH, and N, P, and K content. A better practice is to send soil samples away to local labs (often universities' cooperative extensions provide this service for a small fee), which will test for a wider array of conditions and send back a complete analysis along with a list of recommendations for soil amendments, fertilization, and pH adjustment. It is beneficial to take several samples (10 or more) within areas of the site that have similar conditions (slope, vegetative type, etc.) with a clean tool, such as a spade, and mix those small samples into one. Samples should be taken to a depth that is below major roots (4-6" in turf areas and up to 8" in shrub or tree beds). It is helpful to take samples a few months prior to plant installation in order to provide ample time to adjust pH, if necessary.

Soil pH can be modified with the addition of sulfur or aluminum sulfate to lower pH or lime to raise pH. Both are applied to the soil in weight per surface area (pounds per 10, 100, or 1,000 square feet) immediately after the growing season (generally in fall). While such applications are fairly common practice, it is difficult to change soil pH, especially to increase it, to any great extent.

A more sustainable practice is to apply biostimulants to the soil in order to increase soil microbial activity or stimulate plants to function more efficiently. Biostimulants are organic materials that can enhance plant growth and development and can be composed of a variety of microorganisms, plant extracts, enzymes, plant hormones, or sometimes plant growth regulators. These organic amendments potentially reduce the need for fertilizers or pH adjustments.

Soil tests also screen for the presence of contaminants, including heavy metals. Many urban soils have varying levels of contaminants that prevent healthy plant growth. Soluble salts, especially deicing and fertilizer salts, are of particular concern because of their impact on the movement of water into and out of plant cells, or osmosis. Current standards list a soluble salt content of 600 ppm as a cautionary level and 1,000 ppm as a dangerous level (Watson and Neely, 1994). Likewise, an array of other contaminants, including heavy metals, ammonia, and pesticide residue, can also be toxic to plants as well as to animals and humans and should be bioremediated prior to plant installation. Bioremediation is the process of removing contaminants from soil using a combination of techniques, such as the application of microorganisms,

fungi, enzymes, heat, and even certain plants (phytoremediation) that are uniquely able to take up the contaminants within their cells and degrade, immobilize, or otherwise convert them into less pollutant materials. While some bioremediation processes require the physical removal and transport of the soil to a facility that can process it (*ex situ*), more practices today are applying treatments *in situ*, or in place, because it is less disruptive to the environment and generally less costly.

Perhaps the most widespread and critical problem with urban soils is compaction. Soil compaction destroys soil macropores, which hold oxygen, and increases micropores, which hold water too tightly and make it unavailable to plant roots. Drainage and oxygen diffusion are reduced, and the natural structure conducive to root penetration is destroyed.

Compaction can occur in many ways, most obviously during construction, when soils are purposely compacted to support foundations and pavement bases. Often soils immediately surrounding these structures also become compacted and must be treated before plantings are installed. But soil compaction can also occur unintentionally from pedestrian foot traffic, vehicular traffic, or heavy construction equipment and debris (Figs. 2.10, 2.11).

Several treatments to ameliorate the effects of compaction have been tested to determine their usefulness. Some success has been associated with the incorporation of lightweight aggregates, such as fly ash or expanded slate, into soils prior to plant installation. If compaction is identified after plants are already established, trenching and installing a perforated pipe or drainage mat within the dripline of the plant has shown some promise, as it can increase oxygen and water movement. Another treatment that has demonstrated some success is the use of an excavator or soil aerator to help loosen compacted soil after construction but prior to plant installation (Watson and Neely, 1994). A Cornell University research team, including an ecologist, a horticulturalist, and a landscape architect, has developed yet another treatment: a structural soil product in which large (¾"–1½"), angular, crushed stone—which provides structural stability and an open matrix of pore spaces—is mixed with a clay loam soil with 2–5% organic matter—which provides nutrient and water-holding capacities as well as microbial support. The mixture is held together with a nontoxic hydrogel tackifier and supports the structural requirements of landscape installations as well as the biological requirements of plants (Bassuk, Grabosky, and Trowbridge, 2005).

The most effective way to remedy soil compaction is to prevent its occurrence altogether. When working on construction sites, designers need to specify staging areas that are sufficiently distant from sensitive areas such as mature tree root zones, wildlife habitat, wetlands, future planting beds, and other open spaces. Try to ensure that contractors keep equipment away from these areas and remove debris often. Sensitive areas should be fenced in and not merely covered with mulch or gravel, as the latter has been shown ineffective at protecting soils from compaction.

Likewise, designers should be cognizant of pedestrian desire lines on sites. Pedestrians are notorious for cutting through open areas in order to take the shortest path from point A to point B. Even if a designated

2.10 Foot traffic creates soil compaction near delicate tree roots. (Photo by Adam W. Turner.)

2.11 During construction, heavy equipment can cause compaction of soil that can be detrimental to plants. (Photo by Adam W. Turner.)

walkway exists, pedestrians will cut across lawns and areas of low vegetation. Over time a footpath of compacted soil (called a "desire line") develops that prevents grass and root growth and may become detrimental to existing mature trees. Designers can either design and install more effective deterrents to keep pedestrians, vehicles, and construction equipment away from sensitive areas—since reestablishing original soil structure is almost impossible—or incorporate these desire lines into the overall circulation design of the site.

In specifying soils, designers should be as thorough as possible. Topsoil should be defined in terms of particle size distribution ("sandy loam" based on the USDA classification system), debris (screened and free of plant roots, stones, and other particles over 2" diameter), organic matter content (5%), pH (6.5–7), nutrient content (in ppm of macro- and micronutrients based on specific plant requirements and soil test), and soluble salt and contaminant content (tolerances listed in ppm). Specifications should also include requirements for soil amendments, if deemed necessary by a soil test. For example, designers may specify biostimulants, agricultural- grade limestone, commercial-grade aluminum sulfate, commercial- grade fertilizer derived from synthetic or organic sources, and organic compost derived from mature leaf compost or mature composted animal manure that meets the requirements of the EPA and any state guidelines. These specifications should be site specific, depending on present and future plant coverage, microclimate, and the results of any soil tests.

Importing topsoil is becoming less of an option as natural resources become increasingly scarce and sources of topsoil decline in quality, so remediation of soils in place by screening, bioremediation of contaminants, and addition of amendments and microorganisms needs to become the standard for the industry. When topsoil is to be delivered to the site, however, it is important to request two or more representative samples prior to delivery for testing and comparison to the delivered soil.

## PESTS AND DISEASES

Pests and diseases are opportunistic organisms. They generally only infest or attack plant tissue if the plant is already stressed by abiotic (nonliving) factors such as toxins, salts, compaction, too much or too little water, or extremes of temperature—any of the conditions commonly found in urban environments.

Diseases are caused by microscopic biotic (living) organisms such as fungi, bacteria, and viruses that interfere with a plant's normal structure and function. The four elements necessary for disease development are a susceptible host, a pathogen, a favorable environment, and time. Designers can generally control one or more of these elements by selecting plant species or cultivars that are resistant or less susceptible to particular pathogens, by selecting healthy plants in the nursery, or by avoiding the creation of an environment where disease can flourish. This includes designing an environment where plants will have ample space above and below ground for roots and branches to spread and have sufficient air circulation, sunlight exposure, and access to water and nutrients, as well as situating plants where environmental stresses such as solar reflection, compaction, and vandalism will be minimal. Designers can also recommend maintenance practices to include the removal of infected portions of plants, proper pruning, watering and fertilization, avoidance of mechanical damage, and application of organic controls.

Pests are larger biotic organisms—insects and vertebrates such as moles, voles, rats, squirrels, rabbits, and deer—that cause mechanical damage that can be either aesthetically displeasing or detrimental to the health of the plant (Fig. 2.12). When pests destroy or remove too many leaves (defoliation), the plant can no longer produce enough food energy through photosynthesis to support itself. If an animal removes the bark

of a plant and the tender conductive tissue immediately beneath it, both the outer protective covering and the means for the plant to transport minerals and sugars become lost, especially if the damage encircles the entire trunk; this can cause the eventual demise of the plant.

Designers can be key to helping prevent these pest problems by anticipating them early in the design process and creating responsive design modifications, such as raised planting beds, fencing, diversions (providing alternate food sources), or encouraging natural predators by providing appropriate habitat. This requires an understanding of the life cycle and behaviors of the pest, or identification of its natural predators. Designers can also recommend maintenance practices to include IPM (Integrated Pest Management), which relies heavily on regular assessments of plant health, mechanical removal of pests or damaged plant material, use of barriers, introduction of natural predators, and organic sprays as opposed to chemical controls.

2.12 Insects can damage leaves and cause harm to the plant.

## URBAN WOES

Urban environments present a host of issues and opportunities that do not exist in suburban and rural environments. While designers can take advantage of the varied city microclimates created by certain arrangements of walls and buildings and create conditions conducive to selecting more tender plantings, we must also be aware of the detrimental effects the urban environment can have on plants. Urban conditions can be challenging to plant material in much the same way that city life can be disagreeable to human beings: pollution, increased temperatures, wind tunnels, and mechanical damage are a few of the factors that make urban environments challenging for sustaining plant life.

As we have seen, plants utilize hormones to respond to environmental conditions and to regulate their internal functions. Plants have a unique ability to respond to drought conditions by closing their stomata and preventing further water loss, to sense shortened day lengths and respond by moving water out of their cells before winter sets in and potentially causes cell rupture by freezing, and to sense high temperatures and respond by emitting proteins that prevent heat shock. The extent of the response determines the tolerance of the plant to a given condition, which means that some plants are better able to survive in that condition than others, although there are limits to the tolerances of plants.

Although we do not usually have direct control over difficult urban conditions, we can respond to them in two key ways: arranging design elements to protect plants from harsh conditions and taking extra care in species selection. Plants that are tolerant of dry, windy, salty coastal conditions—such as *Juniperus*, *Ilex glabra*, *Rosa rugosa*, and Platanus x *acerifolia*, to name just a few— are generally also more tolerant of urban conditions, which tend to be similar. Species adapted to swamp environments can also be effective urban choices since they are tolerant of the lack of oxygen that accompanies soil compaction.

## POLLUTION

Pollution is harmful to plants in a variety of ways. Directly, pollution in the form of particulate matter can damage leaves by causing burning, blocking of stomata, and scattering of incoming light. When light is less available to plants and blocked stomata prevent the exchange of gases, metabolic processes such as photosynthesis are reduced and plants fail to thrive. Similarly, particulate matter can create acidification of rainwater, which can also cause burning of leaves and other aboveground portions of plants as well as a decrease in soil pH, rendering nutrients unavailable.

Indirectly, pollution is resulting in the depletion of our ozone layer, causing more UV light to reach the earth's surface. UV light damages not only skin but also plants and wildlife. Air pollution in the form of greenhouse gases (carbon dioxide, methane, nitrous oxide, etc.) that are created by burning fossil fuels is increasing air temperatures globally and leading to a host of problems not only for plants, but for all life on earth.

## INCREASED TEMPERATURES

Infrared maps of land masses show urban areas that are several degrees warmer than outlying suburban and rural areas; in fact, urban areas may be a full USDA hardiness zone warmer than neighboring towns. This phenomenon, termed urban heat islands, is caused by the acres of heat-irradiating surfaces that comprise our cities.

For some regionally native plants, these increased temperatures may prove intolerable; in response, we may need to expand our search for appropriate natives to warmer regions of the country and learn to shift our plant palette to accommodate these higher temperatures.

Likewise, solar reflection from adjacent buildings can also increase temperatures, not only in summer but also in winter. Plants exposed to these short bursts of higher temperatures during winter, when they are dormant, can suddenly begin "awakening." Leaves may begin to transpire while water is still frozen in the ground and unavailable, causing drought stress, buds may begin to open, only to be killed by frost, and other metabolic processes may begin that create vulnerabilities when temperatures once again dip below freezing.

At the same time, plants installed in the shadow of tall buildings may not receive the sunlight required for photosynthesis and may struggle. The urban built environment can complicate our usual approach of planting sun-loving plants along the southern exposures of buildings and shade-loving plants in northern or eastern exposures or under building canopies. Buildings greatly affect not only temperature but also light levels and thus must be factored into our site evaluations and consequent plant choices.

## WIND TUNNELS

Our cities are made up not only of acres of impervious, heat irradiating surfaces, but also of labyrinths of tall buildings, which channel air and create wind tunnels where winds may be at such high velocities that tall trees cannot support themselves. Staking may be required to prevent the liability of toppling canopies and falling limbs. Plants—particularly broadleaf evergreens—may also suffer from wind damage and may require spraying with antidessicants (a waxy coating that prevents too much water loss) or the application of other physical protection such, as wrapping with burlap during winter months. In these windy microclimates, designers should strive to plant wind- tolerant plants, which tend to have smaller leaves and sometimes a waxy coating—plants such as *Juniperus*, *Sedum*, *Crataegus*, *Gleditsia triacanthos*, or *Rosa rugosa*. Both wind-tolerant plantings and built structures can act as windbreaks to protect less hardy plants on the leeward side.

## MECHANICAL DAMAGE

Another common problem in urban areas is the interaction between humans and plant material. Mechanical damage can occur from vandalism or from maintenance equipment such as weed whackers, lawn mowers, and vehicles (Fig. 2.13). Plants can sometimes successfully respond to this damage by programming the death of cells in order to "wall off" damaged areas, creating a barrier between damaged and live tissues and protecting the plant against attack by microbes; however, this defense is dependent on the extent of the damage and the health of the plant. Designers can help prevent mechanical damage by designing broad mulch or plant beds beneath trees to keep maintenance crews from driving equipment or running weed whackers too close to trunks, by providing paved areas along pedestrian desire lines in order to prevent foot compaction near delicate roots, by utilizing plants with natural defenses, such as spines or thorns, in areas where vandalism is problematic, and by providing comprehensive maintenance plans that anticipate and help prevent these situations.

The best way to avoid problems in the landscape is to select the right plant for the environment from the beginning. Our basic understanding of plant biology and plants' cultural requirements, together with a comprehensive study of the site's unique microclimate, will inform appropriate plant selection. The establishment of a comprehensive maintenance plan, outlined in Chapter 7, will help ensure that the landscape will continue to remain healthy and express our design over time. In the next chapter, we consider how plant forms and features can be used to expand our plant palettes.

2.13 Beech trees are easy targets for vandalism thanks to their smooth bark. (Photo by Adam W. Turner.)

# 3

## MORPHOLOGY: SPATIAL AND VISUAL CHARACTERISTICS OF PLANTS AS DESIGN FEATURES

Designers are visual people. The lines that we draw in two dimensions represent objects in three dimensions, and our mind's eye sees the culmination of these lines before they are constructed. They exist only in the creative hubs of our brains until the first shovelful of earth and the first swing of a hammer are executed. As professionals, it is our responsibility to understand the characteristics and qualities of each material we specify. We often find inspiration in the array of available products, utilizing them in ways that highlight particular design features. Just as a select grade of lumber should be carefully chosen to enhance an entryway, a row of cabinets, or a detail of furniture, so too should a particular species of plant be carefully chosen to highlight that same entryway, provide a backdrop to an intimate seating area, or frame a spectacular vista.

Design is perhaps most informed by our perceptions of plants' spatial and visual characteristics, which are based on the plants' morphology. As spatial elements in design, plants help define and create spaces much in the same ways that walls, ceilings, hallways, gateways, floors, and windows do, regardless of their changing forms over time (Fig. 3.1). In this way, planting design plays a key role in integrating buildings and other structures into their environment. Plants can soften the scale of buildings, draw attention to particular architectural features, repair and help re-create natural ecosystems, and define comfortable and aesthetically pleasing environments for human beings.

As we study the spatial characteristics of plants and their functions botanically, we come to utilize plants better as design features, taking into consideration their unique habits or forms—including size at maturity, foliage densities, and

GATEWAY
WALLS
CEILINGS
WINDOW

FLOOR

3.1 Plants define and create spaces in the landscape just as walls, ceilings, and floors do indoors.

branching habits, which affect their texture—and other aesthetic details, such as leaf shape and pigmentation, flower and fruit characteristics, bark, and fragrance.

## HABIT

The habit of a plant is its shape and size, or the three-dimensional way in which it grows and occupies space. A plant's habit informs how it can be used to direct or inhibit both physical and visual movement through a given space. Because plants are living and growing, their forms often change quite drastically over time; we can anticipate those changes by understanding their habits. For example, many evergreen trees are conical when young but mature into more open forms. Keeping in mind the average size and shape of such plants at maturity, we can design with the mature landscape in mind. If we neglect to consider the sizes of plants at maturity, the result can be the need for severe pruning or removal of plants as they outgrow their spaces.

We should also be aware of the growth rate of a plant, or how long it will take for the plant to reach its mature size. Some plants, such as *Fraxinus*, *Salix*, *Forsythia*, and *Buddleia*, grow rapidly, sometimes adding as much as 6-8' of height in one year, while other plants, such as *Acer palmatum*, *Pinus mugo*, *Buxus microphylla* ssp. *Japonica*, and many dwarf cultivars and varieties, are very slow growing. A slow growth rate can be a desired characteristic for some gardens where maintenance capacity is low, space is tight, or conditions are poor, as these plants typically tolerate lower levels of nutrients and water. A fast growth rate can be desirable where screening is necessary or where the client wants the landscape to fill out within a couple of seasons.

A plant's habit is a direct result of both the plant's predetermined and its environmentally influenced programs to survive; environmental factors such as wind, nutrients, and sunlight can have an enormous effect on the growth of a plant. In order to have the best chance at survival, plants must have efficient exposure to sunlight, especially in the context of neighboring plants. Plants occupy different levels above the ground surface, which allows them to coexist by growing above or below one another. They spread horizontally and fan out their leaves in order to capture the most sunlight possible, and they form a dense or sparse canopy and branching habit in order to help them obtain the proper amount of sunlight needed to produce the food energy required for their survival. Designers utilize this branching or canopy density in order to manipulate the amount of shade provided to a space, or to create interesting contrasts between light and shadow on the ground plane (Fig. 3.2).

## FORM

We can also utilize the overall form of the plant to execute certain functions, such as screening, softening the scale of a building, creating rhythm and unity, or drawing attention to a space or feature in the landscape.

Plants can take many different forms, depending on their genetic makeup and environmental conditions. Prostrate plants, such as *Juniperus horizontalis*, *Vinca minor*, and *Cotoneaster horizontalis*, spread or creep along the ground and can enhance the topography of the land, drawing attention to this feature (Fig. 3.3). These plants also provide important erosion control, especially on

3.2 Branching habits create interesting patterns of light and shadow on the ground. (Photo by Adam W. Turner.)

3.3 Cranesbill Geranium is an example of a prostrate plant.

steep sites, and can be used as underplantings beneath taller plants, creating a pleasing overall composition. Clumping and rounded plants, such as *Rhododendron*, *Hydrangea*, and *Coreopsis*, and oval and upright plants, such as *Pyrus calleryana* and *Tilia cordata*, tend to soften the feeling of a landscape. They can be used to define an edge in an unobtrusive manner, as along a pathway or foundation of a building, providing scale and interest while blending hard architectural lines (especially when similar forms with varying heights are planted in combination; Fig. 3.4). Bunching plants, such as ornamental grasses, which originate from a tight bunch and arch outward, and weeping plants, such as *Prunus subhirtella* and *Salix alba* 'Tristis', are generally used as accents, either helping to create a restful feeling in the landscape or, conversely, acting as a focal point or exclamation (Fig. 3.5). Weeping plants also draw the eye downward toward the ground (Fig. 3.6). Conical plants, such as *Ilex* x *meserveae*, *Quercus palustris*, and *Picea pungens*, which taper from the base to a sharp apex, and fastigiate plants, such as *Ilex crenata* 'Skyrocket' and *Quercus robur* 'Fastigiata', which are narrow and columnar, can create rhythm within the landscape because they tend to have very regular forms that are reliably replicated from plant to plant (Figs. 3.7, 3.8). These bold, vertical plants can also be used as focal points, drawing attention to their forms, or when planted tightly together can create an effective, uniform screen. A row of similar plants— an allée of *Liquidambar styraciflua*, for example—planted along a line of buildings with vary-

3.4 Rounded plants, like these hydrangea, help soften and define hard architectural edges.

3.5 Plants with bunching and weeping habits, such as this ornamental grass, lend a restful feeling to the landscape. (Photo by Adam W. Turner.)

3.6 Weeping plants, such as these weeping willows, lead the eye downward. (Photo by Adam W. Turner.)

3.7 Dawn redwood is an example of a conical plant.

3.8 These fastigiate street trees create rhythm in the landscape.

ing architectural styles can help create unity. Sculptural plants, such as statuesque palms, succulents such as hens and chicks, and more irregular-shaped plants such as Harry Lauder's walking stick, can also be used as specimens or focal points within a design, often lending a more playful feeling to a space (Fig. 3.9). Finally, horizontally spreading forms, such as *Cornus kousa*, *Viburnum plicatum* var. *tomentosum*, and *Achillea* sp., tend to lend both stability and movement to a design, drawing the eye across the landscape

3.9 Sculptural plants become focal points in the landscape. (Photo by Timothy Sheehan.)

3.10 Horizontally branching plants, like this flowering dogwood, create movement within the landscape. (Photo by Adam W. Turner.)

3.11 Multistemmed ornamental trees provide a shorter, broader massing in the landscape.

(Fig. 3.10). These horizontal forms can also be used to create broad screening.

As designers, we are usually very aware of the lines plant habits draw in the landscape—whether it be the line created by the silhouette of the overall plant or the lines created by the individual branches, leaves, and petals—as the culmination of these lines is what creates movement in space. When we specify plant material for a project, we should provide specifics about the forms we are seeking, especially for species whose forms can be easily manipulated at the nursery.

Some trees, for example, such as *Acer palmatum*, *Amelanchier canadensis*, and *Betula nigra*, can be grown with either a single main leader or with multiple leaders, two very different visual effects in the landscape. If the aim is for the plant to provide broad screening, then a multistemmed tree is best (Fig. 3.11). If the intent is to have a repeating element of singular, uniform, straight trunks, then single-stemmed trees should be specified. Multistemmed "trees" are often considered large shrubs and tend to grow slightly shorter than their single-stemmed counterparts, which may be another reason for selecting them in certain situations.

## TEXTURE

Designers are also concerned with the texture of a plant, its visual roughness or smoothness. From afar, texture is assessed based on a plant's branching habit, or on how large or small the clusters of differentiated branches and foliage appear. At close proximity, texture is determined by the size and shape of the leaves and

3.12 Finely textured plants, such as this yew, are good candidates for clipped forms.

3.13 Coarsely textured plants, such as this magnolia, advance with bold and eye-catching forms in the landscape.

twigs. Finely textured plants are those with small leaves, slender twigs, or smaller clumps of branches and foliage. These plants tend to recede in the landscape, and the overall outline of the plant becomes more prominent. For example, finely textured plants, such as *Taxus*, *Picea*, *Buxus*, and *Ligustrum*, are often used in clipped forms because their individual leaves and twigs do not compete with the desired overall outline (Fig. 3.12). Coarsely textured plants, such as *Catalpa*, *Mahonia*, and *Hydrangea*, have larger leaves, thicker

twigs, or larger clumps of branches and foliage (Fig. 3.13). These plants tend to advance in the landscape, throw bolder shadows, and act as anchors within larger plant groupings. From a botanical standpoint, a more finely textured plant may be better suited to climates where heavy snowfall or high winds are common, as the leaves do not hold as much snow or carry as much resistance and the twigs are more apt to bend than break. On the other hand, a more coarsely textured plant, with larger leaves, may be better suited to surviving in lower layers of a forested environment, where more surface area is needed to catch all available rays of sun.

## SIZE: HEIGHT AND WIDTH

A plant's size is also an important design consideration, but since plants are living, growing objects, designers must resist the notion that the size they are at the time of installation is the size they will always remain. Plants that are spaced too close together at the time of installation quickly run out of space to grow, resulting in plantings that are competing for space and resources and starved for sunlight, nutrients, and proper air circulation; problems such as fungal disease, malnutrition, and pest infestation can occur unless beds are thinned properly. A crowded planting will need severe pruning, which can result in not only aesthetically unpleasant forms but also unhealthy plants. Plants grow and spread in order to most efficiently capture sunlight. Those that are pruned haphazardly are not as efficient in capturing sunlight, and therefore become unable to produce the proper amount of food to survive. Plants that are pruned with little concern for their overall structure often also become prone to downed limbs as their natural stability is jeopardized, presenting a safety hazard to neighboring structures and pedestrians.

In most situations, we need to design with the mature landscape in mind. The size of the mature plant should determine the number and spacing of plants within the design. For example, many rhododendrons will eventually grow to 5–6' width and should be planted a minimum of 5' on center, even if the plants at time of installation are only 2–3' wide. If "instant gratification" is desired in the landscape—that is, if the landscape needs to look full from day one— then we need to communicate to the client the future need to thin plant beds in order to ensure continued health. This thinning out of the mature plant bed should be reflected very specifically in maintenance plans along with tolerances for pruning. For example, designers should describe the number, location, and types of plants to be removed, divided, or transplanted as well as how to properly prune for health while continuing to reflect design intent (i.e., thinning vs. shearing). Or we might recommend, based on our client's budget, to have larger plants installed from the outset. These plants are more mature, and therefore tend to be more expensive. If cost is a factor, we can specify slower-growing plants to be installed at a more mature size, while faster-growing plants can be installed in smaller sizes, helping the landscape grow and mature more consistently while reducing materials costs. We can also

3.14 The designer's intent has been achieved five to eight years after planting this landscape: the cotoneaster is cascading down the fountain wall, the shrubs are separating the patio space from the remainder of the yard, and the clematis is filling out the pergola.

specify appropriate cultivars and varieties that are slower or faster growing, depending upon the desired look three to five years after installation (Fig. 3.14).

Other common mistakes in plant spacing occur with foundation plantings and under utility lines. Shrubs and trees that are planted too close to building foundations can create problems for the structure by enticing insects, especially termites, to feed on wooden members. They can also prevent proper air circulation between facade and plant, creating rot and fungal problems for both (Fig. 3.15). Again, an understanding of the mature plant size informs how far a plant should be spaced from a structure. For example, a shrub that is 4–5' wide at maturity should be planted with its center spaced a minimum of 2.5' away from the structure in order to allow space between the mature plant and the structure. Similarly, trees that are planted beneath overhead utilities can create maintenance problems if utility companies cannot access these structures, or where high winds can topple trees and take utility lines down with them. These trees must be pruned in order to protect the utility lines, often with detrimental results to the plant; proper plant selection is of the utmost importance in these instances (Fig. 3.16). Lower- growing trees and dwarf cultivars and varieties should be selected, and many utility companies and municipalities now provide lists of "approved" or "suggested" species.

Just as plants need the proper amount of

3.15 When trees are planted too close to building facades, they must be pruned more frequently. (Photo by Adam W. Turner.)

3.16 Trees and utility lines seldom get along.

SCREENING
EYE LEVEL

WAIST HEIGHT
KNEE HEIGHT
GROUND LEVEL

3.17 Spatial characteristics of plants.

space above ground, they also need ample space below ground. Plant roots compete with pavements and underground utilities, sometimes cracking and heaving pavement and creating liability concerns. All too often plants are given only a small fraction of the soil volume they need in order to take up the required water and nutrients and also secure their root systems to prevent them from toppling over. A mature tree's root system can extend to twice the diameter of its canopy or greater under natural conditions. A stunted root system can put the plant at risk of malnutrition, wilt, and instability unless supplemental water, nutrients, and protection from wind gusts are provided. Chapter 7 includes a section on the challenges of roots and how to address them.

From a spatial standpoint, plants can be categorized based on their height, which determines to a great extent how they can be used to perform certain functions in the landscape, such as providing scale, choreographing visual and physical movement, and lending balance and unity to a design. Generally, plants are categorized within five different groups, based on their relationship to the height of the human form: ground-level, knee- height, waist- height, eye- level, and screening plants (Fig. 3.17). Note that these categories reference the mature size of the plant.

- **Ground-level plants** are typically less than a foot in height and include mown grass and other sprawling or creeping groundcovers, either herbaceous or woody, such as *Juniperus horizontalis, Thymus praecox, Arctostaphylos uva-ursi, Geranium* sp., and *Hedera helix*. These plants do not obstruct movement and are often used in circulation areas where hard surfaces are not desired as a means of directing or suggesting move-

3.18 Low plantings can be used to paint patterns on the ground.

ment. Similarly, they can be used to enhance topological forms, both flat and sloped, and to "paint" patterns on the ground (Fig. 3.18). They can also provide a link between different areas of a design by visually connecting points of interest, their repetitions creating visual movement in the landscape.

- **Knee-height plants** are typically between 1' and 2.5' tall and include dwarf shrubs and low perennials, such as *Caryopteris x clandonensis*, *Potentilla fruticosa* 'Goldfinger', *Lavandula angustifolia* 'Munstead', and *Calluna vulgaris* 'Silver Knight'. While these plants are not tall enough to completely prevent pedestrians from crossing over them, their height is sufficient to create a psychological sense of boundary while still maintaining a strong visual connection across them. They can be planted beneath or in front of taller plants, creating layers of foliage, or in patterns that are meant to be seen from above, such as from the upper windows of adjacent buildings. Knee-high plants are also useful as a low edge or for containment, establishing visual stability in the landscape by helping to link areas together (Fig. 3.19).

- Waist-height plants are typically around 3' to 4' tall and include small to medium shrubs and medium to tall perennials such as *Clethra alnifolia* 'Hummingbird', *Hydrangea macrophylla* 'Blue Wave', *Rosa* 'Meikrotal', *Hemerocallis* 'Hyperion', *Rudbeckia subtomentosa* 'Henry Eilers', and *Iris sibirica* 'Caesar's Brother'. These plants provide more of a physical barrier but still do not impede visual access or block views or sunlight (Fig. 3.20).

- **Eye-level** plants are typically around 6' tall and include tall shrubs and some very tall, back-of-the-border perennials such as *Rhododendron catawbiense*, *Kalmia latifolia*, Viburnum x *burkwoodii*, *Miscanthus sinensis*, *Alcea rosea*, and *Aruncus dioicus*.

- **Screening plants** are taller still, 8' and above, and include tall shrubs and

3.19 Knee-height plants suggest boundaries without impeding visual access.

3.20 Waist-height plants provide a barrier for a dining terrace.

trees such as *Thuja occidentalis* and *Chamaecyparis obtusa*. Both eye-level and screening plants provide physical and visual barriers and can deter pedestrian movement, act as a backdrop to ornamental plantings, frame views, provide privacy, or buffer visual and auditory noise or an undesirable view (Fig. 3.21).

A plant composition generally includes plants from multiple height categories. For example, an intimate garden space may be edged with dense eye-level plants that not only help define and enclose the space but also provide a backdrop to more visually interesting waist- to knee-height plants. Within this overall garden space, there may be ground-level plants that help direct movement to a bench or focal point that sits beneath a tall screening plant with an overhanging canopy. The canopy helps provide scale to this

3.21 Screening plants provide both physical and visual barriers.

smaller area within the larger garden space and creates a sense of arrival. Taller plant masses within the border edge will help balance the space and give the eye places to rest, while shorter and more consistent plant masses will help draw the eye across the space and provide unity.

Beyond a plant's habit, a number of other morphological characteristics add sensory interest to our designs—leaf shapes, textures, and variegations; colorful blooms; unique fruit structures; and the fragrances of foliage, flowers, or fruit.

## LEAF

The leaf is one of two aboveground, and therefore visible, organs of a plant (the other is the stem). It also tends to be the most abundant, as well as longest-lasting, portion of a plant. Often, when blooms have gone by and fruits have fallen, the leaves remain, sometimes for all four seasons of the year. Therefore, the leaf can be a tremendous asset in the overall composition of a design, providing interesting variations in texture, color, and shape (Fig. 3.22).

The leaf also has tremendous value from a biological standpoint, being primarily responsible for capturing sunlight and exchanging gases, through transpiration, with the atmosphere. The adaptations plant leaves have undergone over millions of years, in order to assist them in survival, are often the very characteristics that make them so interesting to us aesthetically, and these will be described below.

3.22 Clever foliage compositions, such as this garden of needled evergreens, provide long-lasting interest in the landscape.

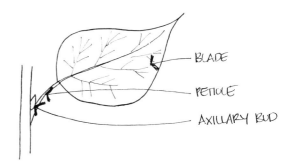

3.23 Leaf anatomy.

## LEAF ANATOMY

Anatomically, the leaf of a plant is usually composed of three major parts: the blade, the petiole, and the axillary bud (Fig. 3.23).

- **Blade**: The wide, flat portion of the leaf that contains chloroplasts; it is typically thin and broad so it can capture sunlight and absorb carbon dioxide in order to carry out photosynthesis. The blade is also responsible for water loss in a plant.
- **Petiole**: The flexible, herbaceous stalk that connects the blade to the stem. The petiole, because of its flexible nature, is designed to rotate the blade throughout the day in order to track the sun's changing position, spread blades out for the most efficient exposure to sunlight, and withstand harsh winds and rains without breaking. Certain plants, such as tulips and lilies, do not have petioles, and are termed sessile.
- **Axillary bud**: The point of new growth that exists at the axil of the leaf, or the angle created between the petiole and the stem. The region where the petiole connects to the stem is called the node, and the space between two nodes is called the internode. These are important areas to be able to identify when pruning a plant, which will be discussed in later chapters.

## LEAF ARRANGEMENT

The manner in which blades are arranged on a leaf and leaves are arranged on a stem is based on their genetic composition, and it is species specific. When a leaf consists of a single blade, it is termed a simple leaf. Examples include *Acer, Tilia, Forsythia,* and *Helianthus.* Sometimes blades are composed of multiple leaflets, and are termed compound leaves. Examples include *Fraxinus, Gledit-*

*sia traicanthos, Rosa,* and *Polemonium caeruleum.* The more leaflets a compound leaf contains, the finer the texture of the leaf, and the more filtered the shade. Compound leaves with many leaflets have more gaps between blades, allowing light to pass down through the plant to the leaves below and the ground beneath and often creating interesting shadow patterns on the ground. The most definitive way to determine if a leaf is simple or compound is to check for axillary buds at the base of the petioles, since these are not present at the base of leaflets, only at the base of leaves.

Compound leaves can be further defined by the arrangement of the leaflets. Pinnately compound leaves have a central axis, with leaflets attached to it at various points, such as walnut (Fig. 3.24). Palmately compound leaves have no central axis, but rather a common point where leaflets attach, like a palm of a hand, such as clover (Fig. 3.25). Leaves are also arranged in various ways on the stem of a plant. Sometimes leaves are arranged opposite one another, or there are two leaves per node on the stem, pointed in opposite directions. Sometimes leaves are arranged in an alternate configuration, where there is only one leaf per node on the stem, but these leaves are still generally pointed in opposite directions one from the other down the stem, in order to be most efficient in light collection. A third variation is a whorled arrangement, where three or more leaves occur at each node and appear to spiral around the stem (Fig. 3.26). These formations are genetically predetermined, as well as species specific, helping plants balance the most efficient capture of sunlight with the least amount of water loss. Knowing the typical arrangements of commonly encountered species can assist greatly in plant identification.

## DESIGN FEATURES OF LEAVES

As designers, we are also concerned with some of the finer, and widely variable, details of leaves that give them the character, texture, and color to enhance our designs.

- **Veination**: Veination is one such characteristic that can have an effect on the texture of a leaf. Veins are the extension of xylem and phloem, which carry water

3.24  Pinnately compound leaf.     3.25  Palmately compound leaf.     3.26  Whorled leaf.

3.27 Oakleaf hydrangea have coarsely veined leaves.

and nutrients from the roots through the trunk and/or stems and become visible in the thinner tissues of the leaves. The arrangement and configuration of these veins affect the appearance of the leaf (Fig. 3.27). Parallel veins—as in grasses, palms, and iris, among others—echo the lines of these plants' linear form, and do not cross. Netted veins, on the other hand, are more intricate roadmaps that either have a central axis, called a midrib, with smaller branches radiating from it—termed pinnately netted, as in Fagus—or branch off a common point, termed palmately netted, as in Acer. The size, thickness, and visual presence of these veins can make the difference between leaves that appear smooth versus coarse, wrinkled, or almost quilted in appearance. In these ways, veination can be used as a design feature, creating patterns in the landscape with lines and textures. Because we need to be in close proximity to the leaf in order to see the veination, as well as some of the other characteristics listed below, their presence can help complement the overall plant composition, taken in gradually as we move through the landscape. These finer details of individual plants can further enhance other more readily visible characteristics of a design.

- **Margin**: The margins, or edges, of a leaf can also have an effect on its character and appearance. A leaf with a smooth margin is termed entire. Leaves may have serrate (toothed), crenate (scalloped), sinuate (wavy), or lobed margins (as seen in maples and oaks), as well as many other variations (Fig. 3.28).
- **Shape**: A leaf's shape can also serve as a design element and contribute to the plant's texture. Leaves can be long and linear, oblong, ovate (egg-shaped), deltoid (triangle-shaped), spatulate (like a spatula), cordate (heart-shaped), and on and on (Fig. 3.29). Large leaves with broad

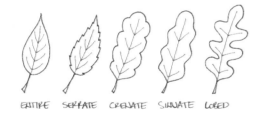
3.28 Leaf margins.

3.29 Leaf shapes.

blades have a bolder texture in the landscape, while those that are smaller and narrower, or have finely serrated margins, have a finer texture. Combining textures within a design creates interest and movement. Linear foliage and/or horizontal branching habits can direct the eye, lacier textures can recede and create a sense of calm, and bolder textures create focus. The harmony or contrast between textures and other plant characteristics contributes to balance, interest, and unity in the landscape (Fig. 3.30).

• **Pigment**: A feature that is perhaps one of the most interesting to designers is leaf pigment. A pigment is any substance that absorbs light. Chlorophyll, a pigment typically present in the greatest quantities in leaves, absorbs mostly red and blue-violet light and reflects green, which is the color we see most clearly. As chlorophyll absorbs red and blue-violet light from the sun, it engages in photosynthesis and allows the plant to convert this solar energy into simple sugars that

may be either utilized for energy or converted into other secondary compounds needed to survive. Other accessory pigments often are present as well, but tend to be masked by chlorophyll. Xanthophylls, which reflect yellow light, carotenoids, which reflect orange light, and anthocyanins, which reflect red light, are typically present in lesser quantities. In temperate climates, as chlorophyll begins its programmed death in the fall in preparation for winter dormancy, these accessory pigments become visible, resulting in the vibrant golds, oranges, and crimsons we see in native temperate climate plants (Fig. 3.31). Similarly, but in a less dramatic way, we also see variations in pigmentation in other plants. Depending on the concentration of particular pigments, some plants' leaves appear more blue-green, chartreuse, bronze, or burgundy throughout the season; these can be utilized as specimens in plant groupings, or can create a subdued backdrop that allows more colorful plants to "pop"

3.30 Combining leaf colors, shapes, and textures provides interest in the landscape.

3.31 Accessory pigments become visible as chlorophyll breaks down in autumn.

3.32 Variations in pigmentation of maples.

3.33 Trichomes often give leaves a fuzzy, silver appearance, as is seen in this lamb's ear.

3.34 Tendrils allow plants to climb up structures.

(Fig. 3.32). Leaves have an extraordinary range of colors to which we, as designers, should be attuned. Much more is discussed with regard to color theory and the use of plant color in design in later chapters.

• **Leaf adaptations**: Throughout millions of years of evolution, many plants have produced unique leaf adaptations to help them survive. Some have fine hairs that cover one side of the blade. These epidermal growths are called trichomes and help regulate temperature (Fig. 3.33). In arid climates, these trichomes are often white or silver in color (affecting the color, sheen, and feel of the leaf as a design feature) and reflect infrared radiation. Alternately, in cooler climates, trichomes can provide extra protection against lower temperatures. Trichomes can also protect plants against pests. Some leaves are coated with an epicuticular wax, which can reduce water loss, keep leaf surfaces drier and thus prevent fungal diseases, or reflect infrared radiation to moderate temperatures. Other examples of leaf adaptations include leaf modifications such as tendrils, threadlike structures that help plants climb in order to gain sunlight or space (Fig. 3.34); bud scales, adapta-

3.35 Bracts, as seen on this kousa dogwood, are often confused with flower petals. (Photo by Adam W. Turner.)

As designers, our choices in combining and contrasting leaf shapes, textures, and colors are what make for interesting and aesthetically pleasing results even when blooms have gone by or fruits have dropped. The foliage of a plant, even in its subtlety, is much longer lasting, and can be used as the persistent design feature, often even in winter months with evergreen and semi-evergreen plants.

## FLOWER

Botanically, the flower of a plant is nothing more than a modified shoot, or stem, bearing adapted leaves that are modified for reproduction. From a design standpoint, however, the flower can be one of the most exciting design features, drawing the eye to a particular space during a particular season, attracting wildlife to a restored ecosystem, or offering a pleasing fragrance (Fig. 3.36). The showiest flowers contain colorful pigments in a myriad of hues, and unique and clever structures that allow them to fertilize suc-

tions to colder climates, which wrap tender buds in order to protect them from cold and water loss and may also contain growth inhibitors that prevent growth too early in the season; bracts, colorful modified leaves that look like petals (and are often confused with them) and attract pollinators to the plant (Fig. 3.35); spines, leaf adaptations that protect plants from pests and can be used in the landscape to deter intruders; and succulents, which often grow in desert or arid climates and have thick, fleshy leaves that act as food and water storage, helping plants survive long periods without rainfall. Succulents can be used in tough urban environments, as well as in roof gardens, which have similar environmental conditions as the plants' climates of origin.

3.36 Flowers provide many exciting design features, including color, beautiful forms, and pleasant fragrances, as is the case with this hybrid tea rose.

3.37 Mountain laurel flowers (*Kalmia latifolia*) have beautiful and fascinating adaptations to promote fertilization: as insects land on the flower, the stamens catapult toward the carpel.

3.38 Cones provide visual interest.

cessfully. For example, the flowers of *Kalmia latifolia* have stamens that catapult toward the carpel when an insect lands within the corolla, projecting pollen in order to fertilize the plant. The flower, which can only be appreciated at close proximity, is fantastically delicate and detailed (Fig. 3.37).

The group of plants within the plant kingdom that produce flowers is called the angiosperms, comprising an enormous variety of species, many in endless variations of cultivars, from trees and shrubs to herbs and vines. From *angio*, meaning vessel, and *sperm*, meaning seed, an angiosperm is a plant that reproduces sexually by forming flowers that contain ovules, which develop into seeds encased within a vessel called a carpel, which then ripens and becomes what is considered the fruit. Alternately, gymnosperms, another large grouping of plants, produce seeds but no fruits or flowers, and include conifers and ginkgo, among others. From *gymno*, meaning naked, and *sperm*,

or seed, these plants also reproduce sexually, but instead of forming seeds within a vessel, they generally form them, exposed, on the leaflike surfaces of cones, which can provide an interesting design feature in and of themselves and will be included in the discussion of fruits later in this chapter (Fig. 3.38).

## FLOWER ANATOMY

The six major structures of a flower are the peduncle, receptacle, calyx, corolla, stamens, and carpel (Fig. 3.39).

- **Peduncle**: The stalk, or stem, on which a flower sits is called the peduncle.
- **Receptacle**: The flower parts that sit atop the peduncle are attached at an enlarged area called the receptacle.
- **Calyx**: The outermost whorl of flower parts that are leaflike, thick, and usually green are called the sepals. Collectively, the sepals are termed a calyx, and their function is to protect the flower during its bud stage.

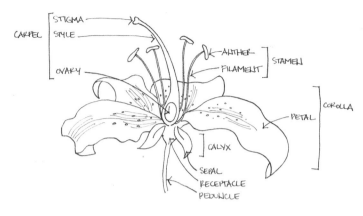

STIGMA

CARPEL | STYLE

OVARY

ANTHER

FILAMENT ] STAMEN

COROLLA

PETAL

CALYX

SEPAL
RECEPTACLE
PEDUNCLE

3.39 Flower anatomy.

- **Corolla**: Inside the calyx is a whorl of petals, which are also leaflike but generally thinner and more brightly colored in order to attract pollinators. Collectively, the petals are called the corolla. Sometimes the sepals and petals are very similar in appearance, or are undifferentiated, as in the case of lilies, in which case the sepals and petals are termed tepals.
- **Stamens**: Inside the corolla is a whorl of stamens, which are the male portion of the plant. The stamen is comprised of a filament, a long, flexible stalk, and an anther, which produces pollen grains.
- **Carpel**: Inside the whorl of stamens is the carpel, sometimes termed the pistil. The carpel is the female portion of the plant and is comprised of an ovary, the style, and a stigma.

## SEXUAL REPRODUCTION

When a pollen grain leaves the anther, it is carried by insect, wind, or some other means of projection to the sticky end of the stigma, where it adheres and germinates into a pollen tube that grows down through the long column of the style and deposits two sperm cells into an ovule within the ovary. Once inside the ovary, one of the sperm cells fuses with the egg to form a zygote, and the other fuses with structures called the polar nuclei to form endosperm, which nourishes the embryo until it can grow on its own. The endosperm is often the portion of the seed that provides humans and animals with a food source as well.

If a flower contains all four whorls of structures (calyx, corolla, stamens, and carpel), it is considered complete. If one or more of the structures is lacking, the flower is termed incomplete. If a flower contains both male and female parts (stamens and a carpel), it is considered perfect and does not require another plant in order to pollinate, but if one of the two parts is lacking, it is termed imperfect and another plant is required for reproduction. If both staminate and carpelate flowers exist on the same plant, that plant is termed monoecious, meaning "one house." Alternately, if the plant contains only male or only female flowers, it is considered dioecious, meaning "two houses." These different types of plants play a role in genetic variability and cross-pollination. Designers should be aware of which commonly used landscape plants are dioecious—hollies, for instance—especially when fruits are being used as a design feature; at least one male plant must be planted within a certain distance of a group of female plants in order to fertilize and produce fruits, so we must know to request this male/female ratio in our plant specifications.

## FLOWER ARRANGEMENT

A single flower or cluster of flowers on an angiosperm is called an inflorescence, and varies widely in composition and appearance from species to species (Fig. 3.40). The main stalk of the inflorescence is termed the peduncle and the secondary, smaller flower stalks that sometimes occur are called pedicels. The way in which these peduncles and pedicels are arranged on an inflorescence determines the flower's texture, linearity, size, and shape. For example, an inflorescence with many pedicels that are relatively long, such as *Astilbe*, is much lacier and more finely textured in appearance than an inflorescence that does not contain any pedicels, such as *Liatris*. The inflorescence of *Liatris* has a single peduncle with florets attached tightly to it, appearing very linear or spikelike

3.41 Yarrow creates a layered, horizontal effect in the landscape.

in form and making a bold statement within a planting arrangement. If the pedicels are arranged so that the inflorescence appears flat-topped, such as *Achillea*, it can have a horizontal appearance en masse, creating a layered effect in the landscape (Fig. 3.41). Finally, inflorescences that contain no pedicels or peduncles, but only a solitary flower called a head, such as *Papaver*, are usually much larger and bolder, and are often valued for the individual characteristics of their petals, tepals, stamens, or anthers, becoming design features in themselves.

From a design standpoint, we should consider all the features of a flower, from its color (not just of the petals or tepals but also of the stamens and anthers) to its fragrance, bloom time, and arrangement or structure. A list of plants with interesting flower features is in Appendix B.

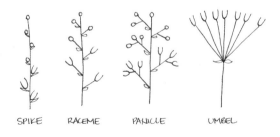

SPIKE    RACEME    PANICLE    UMBEL

3.40 Flower inflorescences.

# FRUIT

Botanically, the fruit of a plant provides the means to pass on its genetic makeup from one generation to the next. But just as with the flower, from a design standpoint the fruit can be a key design feature of a plant (Fig. 3.42). It can attract wildlife to a restored ecosystem, create a focal point in the landscape, and, in some cases, provide a tasty snack. Some of the most interesting fruits are fleshy and colorful, or dry and structural, with unique adaptations that allow them to travel great distances. For a list of plants with interesting fruits, see Appendix B.

## TYPES OF FRUITS

The ripened carpel, or fruit, of a plant is species specific, modified over millions of years to ensure the most successful reproduction of that particular species. Some fruits are able to be carried great distances by wind, water, attachment to the fur of animals, or ingestion and transportation within an animal's digestive tract.

Fruits are classified in one of three categories: simple, aggregate, or multiple.

- **Simple fruits**: Simple fruits are developed from one to several carpels, and are either fleshy or dry.
  - **Fleshy simple fruits** include berries, drupes, hesperidiums, pepos, and pomes. Berries are comprised of one to several seeds, such as blueberries. Drupes contain a stony pit, such as a

3.42 This banana fruit is a bold focus in the landscape.

peach. Hesperidiums are enclosed in a leathery rind that contains oil packets, and include all citrus. Pepos are similar to berries but are enclosed in a thick rind, such as watermelon and pumpkin. Finally, pomes are formed when an enlarged floral tube and receptacle become the flesh; we can often see a secondary ring of tissue within the fruit that differentiates it from the outer skin and encloses the seeds within. Examples of pomes include apple and pear.
  - **Dry simple fruits** are further defined by two categories: dehiscent, in which the walls of the mature ovary break open, and indehiscent, in which the walls do not break open and the seeds remain inside. Examples of dehiscent fruits include milkweed and legumes. Examples of indehiscent fruits include

sunflower, ash samaras, maple schizo-carps, and nuts, including acorns and chestnuts.

- **Aggregate fruits**: Aggregate fruits are formed from a single flower with multiple pistils, where each pistil develops into a fruitlet. Each of these fruitlets matures on a single receptacle. Examples include raspberries and strawberries.
- **Multiple fruits**: Multiple fruits are formed when the fruitlets of individual flowers in a single inflorescence fuse together to make a single large fruit, such as pineapple.

## FRUITS, CONES, AND MAINTENANCE

From a maintenance standpoint, it is important for designers to understand the type of fruit that a particular plant will produce, and how often. Fleshy fruits can often fall from branches, staining sidewalks, patios, or cars, or worse, rot and produce an unbearable stench. Ginkgo trees are a well-known example: female ginkgo trees produce a fleshy cone that, once ripe, smells of rotting flesh; therefore, it is preferable to specify only male ginkgo trees in planting design (Fig. 3.43). Another consideration for designers is the structure of a dry fruit. Sweetgum trees, for example, produce a dry fruit that, while aesthetically interesting, is painful if stepped on with bare feet (Fig. 3.44). Designers may want to avoid planting these trees in areas where either active or passive recreation involving bare feet might occur. Likewise, oak trees can produce multitudes of acorns on alternate years (called "mast years"), creating a tripping hazard along sidewalks or grassy areas (Fig. 3.45).

3.44 Sweetgum fruits can be painful if stepped on.

3.43 The fruits of the female ginkgo exude a tremendous stench that can be avoided by planting only male specimens.

3.45 Acorns can be tripping hazards in the landscape.

Cones can also be a potential maintenance problem. Many gymnosperms produce cones that take multiple seasons to mature, meaning they are held by the tree until they are ripe. These cones can be a prized design feature in the landscape, as they sometimes have interesting structures and pleasant fragrances. But once they mature, they can release a tremendous amount of pollen, which can aggravate allergies and produce a thick yellow dust that accumulates on surfaces. The cones may also drop to the ground and need to be cleared. For all of these reasons, it is important to have a good maintenance plan to avoid any mishaps.

Where low maintenance is desired, it is often common for designers to specify plants or cultivars with persistent (non-dropping) fruit, such as *Malus* 'Prairifire', or plants that will be stripped of their fruit by wildlife before it has a chance to drop, such as *Amelanchier* and *Vaccinium*.

Designers should also have an idea of which plants produce poisonous fruits, especially if we are designing a space that will be enjoyed by children or pets. Many plants produce colorful fruits that may be confused for something edible. Commonly specified plants with poisonous fruits include *Aconitum*, *Robinia pseudoacacia*, *Daphne*, *Delphinium*, *Ilex*, *Digitalis*, *Hedera*, *Ligustrum*, and *Taxus* (Fig. 3.46).

## BARK

The outermost, protective ring of cells in the stem or trunk of a woody plant is called the cork or bark. This outer layer of dead cells can take on many characteristics, depending upon the species of plant. It can be smooth and sinuous, or almost muscular in appearance, rough with deep fissures, or exfoliating, exposing layers of different colors or textures (Fig. 3.47). Bark can exhibit a wide array of colors, adding design interest especially to the winter landscape and in contrast with facades of buildings to create architectural interest. Deeply fissured bark, such as *Diospiros virginiana* or *Acer saccharinum*, can complement other lines in design, or create contrast against opposing textures, heightening the sense of movement within the space (Fig. 3.48). Materials used in building facades, along with the forms of these materials, can be an important contrast to bark. For example, a bronze-barked tree, such as *Acer griseum*, may not look as grand in front of a brick facade as it would against light stone or granite (Fig. 3.49). The light bark of *Betula papyrifera* might be visually lost against a white facade, as opposed to something with a darker hue, such as a brick wall. An annotated

3.46 Yew fruits are poisonous.

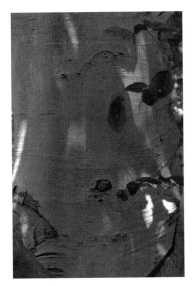

3.47 The bark of a beech tree is smooth. (Photo by Adam W. Turner.)

3.48 The bark of a silver maple is fissured and exfoliating, enhancing the sense of movement in design. (Photo by Adam W. Turner.)

3.49 The bark of a paperbark maple is a beautiful bronze color. (Photo by Adam W. Turner.)

list of plants with interesting bark is provided in Appendix B.

## FRAGRANCE

It is widely known that the center of the brain that processes smell is very closely associated with memory and feeling. Both occur in the limbic system, or the "emotional brain." Therefore, fragrances can evoke emotions and memories that can affect people's moods and provoke powerful responses, both positive and negative, much more so than can color, form, and other qualities.

In medieval times, fragrances from leaves and flowers of plants were often used as remedies for a variety of ailments, from indiges-tion and melancholy to protection against infection and cardiac ailments. Today, we still utilize fragrant plant parts in aromatherapy, but often miss the opportunity to employ them in other ways. While aromatherapy is often concerned with harvested plant parts or oils, fragrance experienced within natural settings can produce a wide range of heightened responses, providing welcome relief to those suffering from ills as diverse as memory impairment (Alzheimer's disease), cancer, or visual impairment, as well as to healthy people who benefit from a connection with nature. The scents from the flowers of lavender, lilac, and rose can lift one's spirit, create a sense of calm, or stimulate memory to recall earlier times (Fig. 3.50). The leaves of some plants, such as *Comptonia*, *Rosmarinus*, and

3.50 Lilacs provide fragrance in the spring landscape. (Photo by Adam W. Turner.)

*Caryopteris*, emit fragrant oils when brushed against; others, such as *Thymus praecox*, produce an aroma when stepped on. Designers can position fragrant plants strategically near windows, along paths, at entrances, in places where people will congregate, or in areas of direct sunlight (since plants often require heat in order to emit their fragrances).

Not all plants produce pleasant fragrances. Some plants, such as *Trillium erectum* and skunk cabbage, produce a foul smell and should therefore be avoided as design choices for most gardens. Other plants are not so easily categorized. For example, the scent of boxwood is very pleasant for some, while others quite literally turn their noses from it. As designers, it is important for us to understand that fragrance can be subjective and that we should use fragrant plants with discretion. Sometimes an abundance of fragrance can be overpowering, in much the way that too much visual stimulation can be overwhelming.

Whether from flower, leaf, or fruit, the fragrance of a plant can be a key element in design, further helping to inform our plant choices. An annotated list of fragrant plants is provided in Appendix B.

The multitude of forms, textures, and structures plants provide offer a rich selection of design features, from the fragrant petals of a rose to the sculptural form of a Japanese maple. Many of these features are particularly interesting because of their colors—whether bright and bold or subtle and subdued. In the next chapter, we take a closer look at how color can be used in design.

# 4

## COLOR IN PLANTING DESIGN

Plants have adapted over years of evolution to present colors that assist them in survival and reproduction. Pigments allow plants to attract pollinators and distributors of their fruit, or deter predators by blending in with their immediate surroundings or imitating a distasteful cousin. They also provide us with abundant opportunities to play with color schemes in order to produce pleasing effects in the landscape.

Everyone has an immediate response, whether subconsciously or consciously, to color. The response might be pleasurable, calming, exciting, disapproving, or uncomfortable, but it is almost always instantaneous. Throughout our evolutionary development we have inherited certain reactions to color that we cannot control—reactions that have assisted us in survival. Likewise, other animals and plants have evolved to react to or don certain colors in order to ensure their

survival and reproduction. For example, the color combination of yellow and black is widely recognized in the natural world as signaling danger. The Io moth, a North American species, reveals startling yellow and black eyespots on its hindwings when under attack in order to deter its predator. Similarly, people know to steer clear of wasps and bees because of their telltale yellow and black stripes. These adaptations and reactions come from centuries of evolution as well as from individual experience.

Throughout history, man has believed in the healing power of color. There is no doubt that colors affect people psychologically and can be manipulated in the environment in order to generate certain reactions. Red, for example, has been shown to be physiologically stimulating, raising both blood pressure and pulse rate and heightening the senses. It is therefore considered a "warm" color. In design, a space filled with bold reds can focus attention and actually increase the perception of temperature, making the body feel warmer. Alternately, the same space filled with "cool" blue tones can have the opposite effect, reducing blood pressure, pulse rate, and brain waves and creating a sense of calm and coolness. As we will see, these characteristics of color can be very useful in design in order to manipulate people's reactions and perceptions of space.

## COLOR THEORY

Reflected light strikes receptors in our retinas and is interpreted by our brains to give us the sensation of color. These sensations are important to the world around us because they help us to distinguish and define our surroundings. In fact, some designers would argue that color is the most significant and meaningful element of a design, but we can add insight to our use of color by understanding better what it is.

Color, in essence, is light energy, or electromagnetic radiation. This energy is defined by ranges of wavelengths that are associated with various colors. The electromagnetic spectrum is a continuum of radiation within which color, or the visible spectrum, makes up a very small portion. Human eyes can only perceive a very limited portion of the electromagnetic spectrum. The wavelength range that can be detected by the human eye is called visible light and occurs between 380 and 750 nanometers (nm), the unit of mea-

sure of wavelengths in billionths of a meter. Visible light is also the range of the spectrum that plants use during photosynthesis, because its energy can be easily converted within plant cells into sugars. Along the electromagnetic spectrum, there are wavelengths of radiation that are shorter and longer than visible light. Shorter wavelengths have higher energy, some of which can damage cells, and include gamma rays, X-rays, and UV rays. Longer wavelengths, which have lower energy, are primarily experienced as heat and sound, and include infrared, microwaves, and radio waves.

Within the visible spectrum lie the colors that we see around us. Each color has a specific wavelength range and is referred to as a pure spectral color, or hue, which contains no white, black, or gray. There are six spectral colors: red (635–700 nm), orange (590–635 nm), yellow (560–590 nm), green (490–560 nm), blue (450–490 nm), and violet (400–450 nm). Because the spectrum is continuous, these colors blend into one another, with no clear boundaries, when light is refracted, or bent, through a prism. When gray is added to a color, it becomes less pure. The addition or subtraction of gray to a hue is called its saturation or intensity, also referred to as a color's dullness or brightness. Alternately, a color's luminosity (its lightness or darkness) is called its value. If white is added to a hue, it is called a tint; if black is added, it is called a shade.

The arrangement of colors within the electromagnetic spectrum has been used to create an illustrative organization of the hues around a circle, showing the relationships

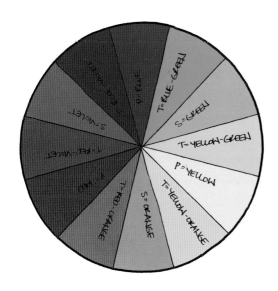

4.1 Color wheel.

that are available to us within the plant kingdom in all the ranges of colors that it presents.

## THE EFFECT OF LIGHT ON COLOR PERCEPTION

Light has an enormous impact on color. Colors tend to look more washed out in full sun, making contrasts subtler at high noon as opposed to dawn or dusk. This is why bold, hot colors look best in tropical and desert climates: these colors are sufficiently saturated to compete with the harsh white light. Warm tones also shine during sunrise and sunset, when the light is more diffuse and warm, reflecting back the warm light. Blues, purples, and whites can glow in the midday sun, but only if they are placed in open shade, where the muted, cool light from the sun and sky can reflect off them. Likewise, cool colors can also glow in the evening, reflecting the cool light of the moon. Under overcast skies, our eyes are able to pick up more subtle contrasts, making colors appear more saturated. For this reason, pastel palettes work well in cooler, misty climates. Designers must keep in mind how a plant composition will look at various times of the day and during various seasons of the year as the light changes.

between colors considered to be primary, secondary, and tertiary. This circular diagram is called a color wheel (Fig. 4.1). A typical color wheel includes blue, red, and yellow as primary colors with corresponding secondary colors (created by mixing adjacent primary colors together) of green, orange, and violet. Tertiary colors are further blends of adjacent primary and secondary colors and include red-orange, red-violet, yellow-orange, yellow-green, blue-violet, and blue-green. Therefore, a basic color wheel contains 12 colors, and further intermediates can be added for a total of 24 colors. We know from experience, however, that there are certainly more than 24 colors in the world, so while this discussion of the color wheel is simplified for the purposes of describing concepts of color, designers must consider the complexities related to pigment and light, as well as the opportunities

## COLOR IN THE PLANT WORLD

Color is abundant in the botanical world, but changes vastly over the course of the seasons, with certain colors more prevalent than others as each season unfolds (Fig. 4.2). Blossoms blanket the landscape in the spring in the range of clear yellows, pinks, purples, and whites before the brighter pinks, yellows, and blues of midsummer take over, followed by the deeper jewel tones—rose, crimson, purple, and gold—in late summer and autumn. While there is almost always an abundance of color in the plant world, flowers and fruits sometimes last mere days. Foliage is longer lasting; fall color converts the prevalent green tones of spring and summer into warm autumn tones that can last a month or more before the canvas of foliage drops and the more neutral browns and grays of exposed bark and the deep greens of conifers and broadleaf evergreens last through the winter months. The subtle but beautiful variations of bark and green foliage can be used in clever and stunning ways to create powerful back-

drops to the more fickle, transitory colors of flowers and fruit. Each of the colors in the botanical world can add unique interest to our designs in the landscape.

In addition to the color changes of fall, foliage comes in a wide range of "base" colors, from chartreuse to deep green to muted red, blue, and silver-gray (Fig. 4.3). It can also provide interesting variegations in tones of cream, yellow, or red, as do many hosta and coleus varieties. Lighter-colored foliage plants, such as *Hakonechloa macra* 'Aureola', *Salix integra* 'Hakuro Nishiki', and *Athyrium niponicum* var. *pictum*, can bring light and interest to a dark garden corner, while blue-tinged leaves such as *Hosta* 'Blue Angel', *Juniperus*, and *Caryopteris* can complement white, pale blue, and purple planting schemes, and offset pale yellows and pinks. Deeper green foliage plants, such as *Rhodo-*

4.2 Pinks and clear yellows enrich this spring landscape. (Photo by Adam W. Turner.)

4.3 The muted red foliage of a Japanese maple complements the apricot poms.

4.4 Silver leaves of lamb's ear complement the pastel yellow *Coreopsis* and purple *Caryopteris*.

*dendron*, *Viburnum*, and *Paeonia*, can create an effective backdrop against which more colorful flowers and fruits will "pop." Generally, darker greens are strong elements in design, while paler greens, including gray-green foliage, appear softer, more fragile. Gray foliage can have an intense effect on other colors, causing both bold and pale colors to brighten. And in itself, gray can change its value based on an adjacent color: gray foliage looks darker next to dark colors and lighter next to light colors (Fig. 4.4). Likewise, lawn areas tend to be lighter green and can intensify other colors surrounding them (Fig. 4.5).

## WHITE

Anyone who has selected white for the walls of a room understands how complex a color it can be; we can select a "white" from a paint palette and be surprised by the amount of pigment that needs to be added in order to achieve that color. Similarly, in the plant world, there are few pure whites. Most are tints of yellow, blue, or green so pale they appear white at first glance. These whites are considered "cool" if the tint is blue or "warm" if of the tint is yellow and generally work best when placed in combination with other colors within the same family. For example, cool whites, such as the blossoms of *Syringa vulgaris* var. *alba*, complement plants in the blue and purple range, while creamy whites, such as *Echinacea* 'White Swan', tend to look best in a grouping of yellows, oranges, and reds (Fig. 4.6). Creamy whites, such as *Clema-*

4.5 The deep green of these yews helps anchor the flower bed and provides a contrast to its whites, silvers, and purples. The lawn area intensifies all the colors of the garden.

4.6 Pure white is rare in the botanical world; often stamens or other floral structures are colored. This white rugosa rose has yellow stamens that would complement other warm tones in the landscape.

*tis paniculata*, can look dingy when placed against a cool-toned white wall (Fig. 4.7).

Because white reflects all light rays, adjacent plantings with softer hues can appear deeper and more contrasting by comparison.

4.7 The creamy/blush tones of these "white" hydrangeas make the fence look pristine and pure white by comparison.

4.8 White glows against a dark background.

White can also soften bolder hues. This can be invaluable in separating blocks or drifts of contrasting colors without overwhelming the eye. But white should not be used indiscriminately, because it is not always a successful buffer between strong, opposing colors, especially when rich contrasts are desired. When placed inappropriately, white can create an incoherent, spotty effect. Also, because of its highly reflective quality, white can be difficult in full-sun gardens, where it can be blinding. White is a good choice, however, for evening gardens and shady areas, as it appears to glow in the darkness and can bring brightness to a dull corner (Fig. 4.8). This can be especially successful when using variegated leaves, such as *Cornus alba* 'Bailhalo', or white bark, such as *Betula papyrifera*, as the foliage effects are longer lasting than flowers (Fig. 4.9).

4.9 Variegated leaves, such as those of 'Ivory Halo' dogwood, are a more long-lasting way to bring white into a design.

## YELLOW

Much like white, yellow is a multipurpose color in the landscape (Fig. 4.10). Golds and brighter yellows complement warm tones such as red and orange, and contrast with deeper tones such as dark purple. For example, a nice late summer combination is *Rudbeckia fulgida* 'Goldsturm' with *Monarda didyma* 'Jacob Cline', *Hemerocallis* 'Chicago Fire', or *Weigela* 'Red Prince'. *Rudbeckia* 'Goldsturm' also makes a stunning contrast with *Salvia* 'May Night'. Paler, more buttery

4.12 Yellow-leaf Japanese maple can provide persistent color in the landscape.

4.10 Yellow is a cheerful color in the landscape. The yellow fall color of an amur corktree brings color to this autumn landscape.

4.11 Use yellow as a focal point in design.

yellows, while still within the "warm" palette, can complement cooler tones, as with *Hemerocallis* 'Flava' planted with *Syringa meyeri* 'Palibin'. Yellow is perceived by the eye most readily, before any other color; it attracts attention and can be used as a strong focal point in the landscape (Fig. 4.11).

Because yellow is so prevalent in the world of flowers and is perceived as such a cheerful color, we often design with yellow flowers in abundance. But we can also call upon yellow foliage plants, such as *Hakonechloa macra* 'Aureola' and yellow-leaf Japanese maple, where longer-lasting yellow hues are desired (Fig. 4.12).

## BLUE AND PURPLE

Pure blue is rare in the botanical world. Among the few plants with pure blue flowers are species of *Delphinium, Salvia, Myosotis, Lobelia,* and *Hydrangea* (Fig. 4.13). Shades of purple, violet, and lilac are more prevalent and can be substituted or used in combination with pure blue. Also, many very attractive plants have blue-toned leaves and needles, such as *Hosta* 'Blue Angel', *Festuca*

4.13 Pure blue is rare in the botanical world.

4.14 Blue foliage plants, such as this 'Elijah Blue' fescue, are another way to provide cool tones in the landscape.

*glauca* 'Elijah Blue', and *Abies concolor,* and are very useful in design, as are the blue fruits of certain species and cultivars of *Viburnum* and *Vaccinium,* among others (Fig. 4.14).

Blues and purples can be pale and luminous, especially when combined with silvery foliage such as *Artemisia, Helichrysum, Santolina,* or *Lavandula,* or dark and seemingly mysterious, especially when they approach black, such as *Tulipa* 'Queen of the Night', *Alcea rosea* var. *nigra, Iris* 'Superstition', and *Aquilegia* 'Black Barlow' (Fig. 4.15). They are considered "cool" tones, lending a calming effect, and can be useful in warmer microclimates, as they give the perception of coolness. Blues and purples also tend to recede in the landscape and are therefore useful in smaller landscape spaces, such as courtyards, and at the backs of the gardens because they give the illusion that the space is larger.

Blues and pale purples complement neutral and cool tones and can complement warm tones when they approach deeper purple. For example, blue cultivars of *Veronica, Delphinium, Syringa,* and *Caryopteris*

4.15 When combined with lavender and silver, blue can be luminous.

4.16 Analogous color schemes using blues and purples make for interesting contrasts.

in the landscape, often requiring some relief for the eye with white flowers, gray foliage, or other neutrals planted nearby (Fig. 4.17). Examples of plants with bright pink flowers include *Astilbe* 'Fireberry', *Azalea* 'Mother's Day', and *Paeonia* 'Tom Eckhardt'. Pale pinks, such as *Paeonia* 'Monsieur Jules Elie', *Spiraea* 'Little Princess', and *Rosa* 'The Fairy', because they are more delicate, are considered neutral in most situations, and can be paired with both warm and cool tones. They also complement brick structures as well as gray facades (Fig. 4.18). These colors tend to

blend well with whites, pale pinks, and pale yellows, while the darker *Buddleia* 'Black Knight', *Syringa vulgaris* 'Monge', *Aconitum* 'Spark's Variety', *Iris sibirica* 'Caesar's Brother', and *Salvia* 'May Night' complement reds, oranges, and golds. These darker hues also make striking contrasts against paler yellows. As a general rule, analogous schemes using blue and purple are easy to accomplish, because the dark and light blues and purples provide ample contrast to keep the garden interesting (Fig. 4.16).

## PINK

Pinks can be either bold and bright or pale and delicate. Bright "hot" pinks have blue undertones and can be bold and stimulating

4.17 Hot pinks often require some white to relieve the eye.

4.18 Pale pinks rarely compete with other colors in the landscape.

pale as distance increases and do not compete with other colors in the landscape.

## RED

Clear reds in the landscape are bold and eye-catching. They advance in terms of depth and can be used as a focal point. Examples of plants with clear red flowers include *Papaver orientale* 'King Kong', *Rosa* 'Don Juan', *Lobelia cardinalis*, *Pelargonium* 'Red Apple', and *Tulipa* 'Apeldoorn', all of which will make a stunning statement in the landscape, but used indiscriminately they can be overpowering (Fig. 4.19). Nature tends to use clear, bright reds in moderation, as do most designers.

While red flowers can be very bold, red fruits and red-tinged leaves and bark tend to be more muted and can complement other colors. Examples of plants with red leaves are many varieties of *Coleus* and *Heuchera*, *Pennisetum setaceum* 'Rubrum', *Cotinus coggygria* 'Royal Purple', *Physocarpus* 'Diablo', and many varieties of *Acer palmatum* and *Weigela*. These plants, because of their more

4.20 Red foliage can create interesting patterns in the landscape.

muted tones, can be used to create interesting contrasts, repetitions, and patterns in the landscape without overpowering a design, and in this way help unify a space (Fig. 4.20).

## GREEN

The peak radiation of the sun is around 500–550 nanometers (nm), which is the color green. The human eye evolved, responding to these light wavelengths, with a unique set of photoreceptors that are most sensitive to green, making it a restful and neutral color. The most prevalent color in the landscape is also green, as chlorophyll is essential to

4.19 Clear reds, like this poppy, can be used as focal points.

plants' survival, yet the subtle variations in foliage colors are immense and can be cleverly manipulated in landscape spaces. Many garden designers consider their designs a success if the foliage or "greens" alone are balanced and unified and do not rely on other colors to complete the effect (Fig. 4.21). These compositions rely on subtle differences in hue as well as line and texture.

Green can also act as a "rest" in a bed of abundant color, providing a buffer between areas of bolder, more contrasting colors (Fig. 4.22). Because it is so abundant in the botanical world, green should be among the first colors we consider in planting design.

4.21 This garden relies on foliage alone for the effect.

## COLOR THEMES IN PLANTING DESIGN

Color preferences tend to be extremely personal. While some people respond favorably to spaces filled with reds, oranges, and yellows, others find these warm color schemes overwhelming. Likewise, some might enjoy the contrast of blue and orange, or red and pink, while others find these combinations unpleasant (Fig. 4.23). Therefore, color preferences should be among the first questions asked of a client, well before specific plant selections, hardscape materials, or exterior paint color selections are made. But as designers we have the opportunity to suggest other creative combinations; I have had more than one client request a garden with a specific color scheme, only to delight later in my suggestion of something new and surprising— a chartreuse hakonechloa in a sea of blue and lavender, or a blue-leaved hosta tucked within a bed of white. While variety is often desired within a planting scheme, we must be

4.22 Lawn helps to intensify bold colors, but also acts as a buffer between colors.

4.23 Some people enjoy the contrast of these complementary colors in the landscape, but others may not.

of silvery-green or by creamy white flowers. Manipulating contrasts in color is an excellent way to create accent and emphasis in the landscape. Likewise, areas of lighter colors can be surrounded by regions of darker, and vice versa. For example, a cluster of pale yellow roses will look outstanding within a mass of *Caryopteris* 'Dark Knight' and help balance dark and light as well as cool and warm tones. By spacing these bursts of varying colors at regular intervals, we create a rhythm in the landscape. We can also create masses that are spaced periodically across the space to provide balance and repetition (Fig. 4.24).

As a general rule, larger masses of color read better than smaller, more segmented dots. Planting in larger drifts also allows colors to touch and change as they come into proximity with other colors. In this way, we can create color sequencing in the landscape. For example, a perennial border that begins with pale yellow *Coreopsis*, peach *Hemerocallis*, and apricot *Potentilla* can gradually build into terra- cotta *Achillea*, and orange *Geum* and *Asclepias* before finally terminating in a mass of intense red *Monarda*. It is important to remember that colors are never perceived in isolation, but are influenced by others that surround them and change with varying distance and light. The red *Monarda* in this example will appear warmer in combination with the other yellows and oranges within the border, but if substituted for deep purple *Iris ensata*, the hue will take on an increased intensity in contrast with the warm colors adjacent to it.

Color theorists have identified thousands

careful to avoid overstimulation by using too many colors or by mixing pale and bold colors together, for example golden yellow *Forsythia* with pale lavender *Rhododendron*.

The design challenge, therefore, becomes balancing unity and complexity, as well as contrast and harmony, in the landscape. One way to achieve this is to incorporate bands, drifts, or blocks of brighter or more contrasting colors within larger areas of less intense, more neutral colors. For example, a mass of hot pink peonies will be emphasized when surrounded by foliage plants in hues of recommendations to assist people in combining colors in a pleasing way. These include, at the simplest, monochromatic schemes, complementary schemes, analogous schemes, analogous-complementary schemes, split-complementary schemes, double-complementary schemes, triads, and tetrads.

- **Monochromatic schemes** are based on one hue that is varied in value and saturation.
- **Complementary schemes** combine hues directly opposite one another on the color wheel.
- **Analogous schemes** utilize colors adjacent to one another on the color wheel.
- **Analogous-complementary schemes** involve two colors next to each other on the color wheel, combined with the complement of one of them.
- **Split-complementary schemes** begin with one color and add the two hues adjoining its complement.
- **Double-complementary schemes** include two closely related hues plus their complements.
- **Triads** and **tetrads** combine three or four colors equally spaced on the color wheel.

Complementary colors and are considered by some to be the basis of harmonious design because the human eye seeks out a

4.24 The regular spacing of these chartreuse and red foliage plants provides repetition in the landscape.

color's complement naturally. If we stare at a color, for example red, long enough and suddenly look at a white surface, we will see a patch of complementary color, in this case green. This phenomenon is called afterimage, or the fatigue effect. The eye requires any given color to be balanced by its complementary, and if the complementary is not present, the eye, or rather the brain, will generate it.

For designers, this afterimage can be an important consideration. In interior design, it is the reason why surgical units often have green walls, in order to give the eye some respite after surgery, and restaurants seldom have red walls and white plates, else the food they serve may look greenish. In planting design, we can provide regions of complementary colors within areas of a solid, monochromatic palette in order to help draw the eye across a space. For example, clusters of yellow *Coreopsis* 'Moonbeam' within a purple-blue bed of *Caryopteris*, *Geranium* 'Johnson's Blue', *Campanula*, and *Nepeta* provide a natural resting place for the eye. By manipulating the spacing between these masses of yellow, we can create rhythm and repetition in the landscape.

In the natural world, however, the "rule" of complementary colors is not so cut-and-dried, because pure hues are not as prevalent in nature. Most flowers, fruits, leaves, and bark have variations in color, such as pink petals with yellow stamens, or orange fruit surrounded by green foliage, and sunlight creates further natural variations in color. Since expanses of pure color in nature are

rare, so too is the eye's insistence on complementary colors in the landscape.

Analogous color schemes can provide a softer, more harmonious feeling in design. These schemes are often found naturally in the landscape, such as in the reds, oranges, and yellows of autumn foliage, and can be quite pleasing to the eye (Fig. 4.25). We will usually find swaths of "warm" or "cool" colors within one region, but rarely a combination of the two. At the Abby Aldrich Rockefeller Garden on Mt. Desert Island in Maine, Beatrix Farrand created a kaleidoscope of colors by designing a mirror image of warm and cool

4.25 Analogous color schemes can be harmonious: this scheme is based on autumnal hues.

tones along the axis of a central lawn—on one side of the lawn lie cool pinks, pale yellows, and lavender-blues, and on the opposite side scarlet, gold, and orange. Farrand sprinkled both sides with white, and added some strong blue tones to the "hot" side for emphasis and unity. Her interpretation of the "rules" of color theory and keen eye for color continue to influence designers.

All of these concepts are important to designers because they help create contrast. Contrast, whether bold or subtle, may be used in design to emphasize areas of importance or create harmony and balance within a space. For example, high contrast can be accomplished in the landscape by using complementary colors; adding a few purple flowers within a bed of mostly yellow flowers and foliage draws attention and emphasis to a space. Similarly, a deep red foliage plant in front of a light- colored wall is another way to punctuate a space. Not all contrasts need to be bold, however. By manipulating value and saturation—by using pink with red, or bright yellow with softer yellow, for example—subtler contrasts can be created that can help harmonize or unify a space.

In landscape and garden design, again, it is often better to keep color schemes simple, especially since green is the predominant color and can make more complicated schemes difficult. That said, designers are known for being creative, using surprising combinations of color with very successful outcomes. The cultural requirements of plants must always be considered paramount, however; plantings will not look right if the plants originate from widely differing habitats, and plants will more than likely perish if their cultural needs are not met.

## CONSIDERATIONS WHEN PLANNING A COLOR SCHEME

When planning a color scheme for a landscape design, it is important to consider the colors of the surrounding hardscape—building facades, paving, paths, walls, and other structures in the landscape—as these colors will most likely not change in the short term. For example, if high contrast is desired in the landscape, a purple-leaved *Cotinus coggygria* may not be as striking a choice in front of a brick facade as would be a *Salix integra* 'Hakuro Nishiki'.

It is also important to consider the seasons during which a particular landscape area should look its best and select plants to enhance those times. Garden spaces adjacent to buildings and visible from windows year-round should provide four-season interest: a flush of blossoms in spring, interesting foliage textures and flower colors in summer, fall color and fruit, and interesting bark combined with evergreens in winter. Gardens that will only be experienced at particular times of the season should present themselves best during periods of peak traffic, providing a flush of color at that time of year. Landscape spaces with little to no access in winter months, such as a summer home that will not be visited between November and April, may not require many evergreens or plants with particularly interesting bark or berries, whereas a ski loft would be enhanced by those winter-interest features. An understanding of the timing and use of the space is important in order to choreograph the best landscape presentation.

The design of color schemes in a landscape is made more challenging by the fact that these schemes change throughout the year. A garden with pale pink *Magnolia* and white *Azaleas* underplanted with delicate blue and purple *Crocus* and buttery yellow *Narcissus* in spring can turn intensely cool in summer with a flush of deep purple *Iris sibirica*, *Hydrangea* 'Mariesii', white *Astilbe* 'Deutschland', and purple *Geranium* 'Blue Blood'. The same garden can gain vibrancy in late summer and fall as late-blooming burgundy *Hemerocallis* complement the autumn leaves of a *Viburnum*, and finally expose the bark of a *Cornus sericea* that contrasts against a blanket of snow in winter. Plant selection is key to the success of these transitions: choosing plants that have flower, fruit, bark, or leaf colors that fit within the color parameters desired for that particular garden or landscape at that particular time.

The direction and distance from which a landscape or garden is approached also affects our planning of color. For example, the dense, low canopy of a *Fagus sylvatica* 'Pendula' can partially conceal the view to an intimate garden space as it is approached down a pathway planted with mostly foliage plants and muted flowers. As the viewer draws nearer, the newly unfolding garden beyond the beech may contain colors more intense than those along the pathway. Likewise, if a garden is meant to be experienced in sequence, a choreography of colors can be arranged to enhance one's journey through the landscape. The color patterns of a space or border may begin with muted tones and eventually shift to bold, bright combinations.

Beyond aesthetics, color can also play a functional role in design. Colors have the power to suggest temperature, extend or reduce dimensions, and provoke stimulation or restfulness. Darker colors can appear heavier and more solid, while lighter colors seem more airy and fragile. Cool or warm colors can alter the effects of temperature and mood. Blues and grays can recede, creating the illusion of distance, while warm colors tend to advance; this can enhance the effectiveness of perspective and focal points, creating spatial deception in design.

Plants provide a myriad of colors from which to choose. An entire garden may be inspired by the deep purple petals of a 'Superstition' iris or the delicate pink of a 'Princess de Monaco' rose. But beyond the aesthetics of plants' various spatial and visual characteristics, landscape design requires us to organize space in functional ways that can solve problems and in creative ways that can elevate our experience of that space. The next two chapters explore how plants' natural features can be utilized to achieve these design goals.

# 5

## PLANTS AS FUNCTIONAL ELEMENTS OF DESIGN

Plants are solid objects in space, with very definite yet ever-changing characteristics; as such, they are design materials, and we can use them effectively to achieve a variety of goals for a landscape. Plants can complement building forms and integrate unrelated building styles, such as the way street trees provide rhythm and unity along a street with buildings of varying architectural styles. They can enhance architectural features by mimicking, contrasting, or drawing attention to forms on facades, and reduce or soften the scale of buildings, creating a more comfortable space for pedestrians to walk or congregate. Plants can provide privacy to windows and courtyards, separating public and private spaces, and define and articulate these spaces by creating outdoor rooms. Sited strategically, plants can even help improve public safety. They can direct views to distant landscapes, screen views away from unpleasant elements, and

frame views to focal points. Designers can also create interest and intrigue in the landscape by using plants to visually manipulate the sense of space, often with the use of hedges.

In addition to these very visual, physical roles, plants can be used to mitigate common environmental discomforts—such as solar radiation, heat, wind, noise, and pollution—to create environments that are more welcoming to both humans and wildlife. These strategies will be more fully explored in Chapter 10.

## COMPLEMENTING, ENHANCING, AND INTEGRATING ARCHITECTURE

Plants are an invaluable asset within the designed environment. They can help extend architectural lines into the landscape, carrying the eye outward and integrating the building with the land. Plants can also complement or contrast with architectural forms and features, enhancing and drawing attention to particular details (Fig. 5.1). Most often plants are selected and arranged to give the feeling that landscape and architecture coexist. For this reason, it is important to survey existing site vegetation early, in order to assess any mature plantings that should be saved or transplanted and identify any new plantings that may be needed. This is of particular importance with older buildings and historic styles of architecture, where the assumption is that both building and landscape have existed for quite some time. These buildings look most appropriate when surrounded by mature plantings and stately trees, such as elms, beeches, and oaks, to help ground the buildings in history (Fig. 5.2).

A study of architectural styles helps in creating a successful landscape composition. For example, contemporary architecture generally employs clean, horizontal lines. These lines can be complemented by plantings with horizontal habits, such as *Acer palmatum* and *Viburnum plicatum* var. *tomentosum*, as well as crisp, structural forms, such as agave, palm, and bamboo, which enhance and extend the lines of the architecture into the landscape. Art Deco tends to be a more vertical architectural style, which can be emphasized by

5.1 Plants can extend architectural lines into the landscape: this hedge mimics the lines of the door.

5.2 A Neoclassical structure set off by the stately trees surrounding it.

5.3 This Arts & Crafts–style building is complemented by loose, informal plantings.

5.4 Upright plants help highlight the entry of this home.

5.5 Conical evergreens can mimic the spires of buildings.

plantings with fastigiate, upright habits, such as *Ginkgo biloba* 'Princeton Sentry' and *Carpinus betulus* 'Fastigiata'. Highly ornamented architectural styles, such as Art Nouveau, Gothic Revival, and Victorian, tend to engage landscapes with more ornate detailing and intricate planting compositions. Victorian structures, in particular, are complemented by "old-fashioned" plantings such as lilacs, mockorange, hollyhocks, and hybrid tea roses, all of which were common plants during the era of that style of architecture. The Craftsman style, including the Bungalow, looks appropriate with unclipped, native plantings and rustic landscape details (Fig. 5.3).

Once plantings are selected to complement the overall architectural style of the building, their arrangement can be determined to highlight particular features. For example, entrances are enhanced by focal plants that

frame. Fastigiate holly or juniper flanking a portico can mimic its columns and draw attention upward to the pediment, further framing the doorway (Fig. 5.4). A small ornamental tree may not be as effective a choice for this type of feature, especially if space is tight and the canopy is broad, as it may hide the portico. But tight, vase-shaped ornamental trees, such as *Prunus serrulata* 'Kwanzan', can be used to flank porticos, as their form, when planted in pairs, creates an inverted V that frames the roofline of the portico. We should consider keeping key architectural features exposed as plants grow and mature. These features can also be mimicked—spires by conical evergreens or columns by tree trunks, for example—but we should also consider contrasting features as a means of creating interest in the landscape (Fig. 5.5). The straight lines of architecture are often

5.6 Streetscapes of varying architectural styles can be unified with trees.

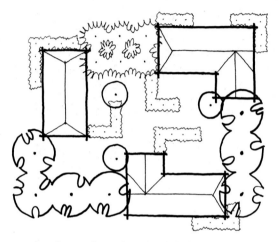

5.7 Plan showing how plants can help link buildings and create space between them.

enhanced when contrasted against the looser organic forms of plant material.

Plantings also help to unify spaces. Street trees are commonly used to unify streetscapes that contain varying architectural styles by providing a repeating element in the landscape and drawing the eye through the space without focusing on the differences among facade styles (Fig. 5.6). In a similar way, plantings can physically and visually link groupings of buildings within a campus setting when they are planted in interconnected masses. In this instance, the plantings not only help unify the buildings, but also subdi-

vide the space between the buildings, creating more intimate outdoor rooms (Fig. 5.7).

## SOFTENING SCALE

Walkways that run along the sides of tall buildings can be uncomfortable places for pedestrians. The contrast between the human scale and that of the building can be so great as to make one feel diminutive. Plantings can be useful in these situations because they can help bring the scale down to a more "human" level. Tree canopies can become intermediate ceilings, blocking the view above and extending the line of the first floor into the landscape (Fig. 5.8). Adding other plantings, such as shrubs and perennials of various heights, can also help bring the scale down and soften the hard, vertical edge of the building.

## PROVIDING PRIVACY AND SAFETY

Plants can be very useful in providing privacy in the landscape, offering an array of color, texture, and fragrance that architectural

5.8 Tree canopies act as intermediate ceilings, extending the line of the first floor into the landscape.

5.9 Plants help to separate private and public spaces.

walls and fences cannot. Plants help define and separate public and private spaces such as dining terraces, sunning decks, and other intimate seating areas, limiting visual access inside and outward (Fig. 5.9). They can also provide privacy to windows by redirecting foot traffic and blocking views while still allowing sunlight to filter through.

Plant characteristics are key to selecting appropriate plants for privacy. Height and density of foliage and branching help determine levels of privacy as much as do quantity and placement. Densely branching shrubs with finely textured foliage, such as *Ilex glabra*, *Ligustrum*, and *Taxus*, tend to provide more consistent coverage than plants with more open habits. Plants with broader leaves,

such as *Viburnum* and *Syringa vulgaris*, also provide effective screening during the spring and summer, but will leave the space exposed in winter once their leaves have dropped.

Plant placement is also an important consideration in efficient screening. Massing plants along all sides of the space provides more thorough coverage than sparse groupings that cover only two or three sides; however, this can leave the pedestrian feeling claustrophobic. Consideration should be given to the extent of screening desired, as well as the degree of enclosure, and its effect on the human psyche. We also need to be cognizant of creating pockets of spaces in public areas where lack of visibility may create safety concerns. Sight lines and views should

5.10 Providing a buffer between vehicle headlights and building windows.

5.11 Deterring pedestrians from entering dangerous or environmentally sensitive areas.

also be considered. For example, if views from overhead windows are to be blocked, then plants with broad canopies, such as *Crataegus viridis* 'Winter King' or *Gleditsia triacanthos* 'Shademaster', should be selected. If views from below need to be blocked because the space is elevated, then shorter screening plants may be sufficient.

Plants can also be utilized to enhance public safety. Often roadways that are East or West facing experience solar glare early or late in the day. This can be ameliorated by trees or other high, dense plantings that block the sunlight. Similarly, streetlights and

headlights can create glare into windows and oncoming traffic (Fig. 5.10). Planting dense buffers along berms and grade changes, or within roadway medians, can help remedy these problems.

Walkways are sometimes positioned along dangerous or environmentally sensitive areas, especially within recreational and campus environments. Plantings can be sited strategically to deter pedestrians away from steep grade changes or prevent them from entering these areas, protecting both people and the environment (Fig. 5.11).

## DIRECTING VIEWS

Plants can be used to direct views toward or away from elements in the landscape. In much the same way they are used to provide privacy, plants can screen unpleasant views of dumpsters, service or industrial areas, and parking lots. In order to effectively screen an element, we identify the line of sight, the height of the object to be blocked, and the distance from the viewer; by cutting a section through the space from viewer to element, we can determine the necessary height of the screening plant. For example, if there is a rising slope between the viewer and the offensive element, a lower planting may be used along an intermediate high point rather than a higher planting along

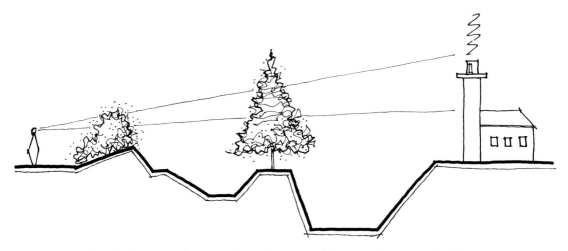

5.12 Topography largely determines the most effective location and elevation of screening plantings.

5.13 Framing views toward distant vistas.

a low point. Also, lower plantings tend to be sufficient when located closer to the viewer, especially if the offensive element is at a distance (Fig. 5.12).

Plants can also frame views toward pleasant scenes, such as beautiful vistas or focal points, by acting as blinders to direct the view toward the desired area (Fig. 5.13). Plants with interesting habits, foliage, flowers, or fruit can also be used as focal points, directing views to the plants themselves.

## VISUALLY MANIPULATING SPACE

We have already looked at the ways in which color can be used to visually manipulate space: cool colors tend to recede and give the illusion of extending space, while warm colors advance and suggest reduced space. We can also visually manipulate space through the massing and arrangement of plants, and especially through the use of hedges.

Hedges, or boundaries formed by a densely planted row of shrubs, trees, or perennials—either clipped or unclipped—have been used since Roman times to enclose fields, provide shelter, contain animals, and bring order to the landscape, often designating property boundaries. Over time, hedges, while still retaining their functional value in defining space, were also intended as aesthetic features in the landscape. Lines of plantings,

combined with human curiosity, tend to draw people through outdoor spaces and encourage them to explore what is beyond. In a similar way that a path leads the eye through space, hedges also create a sense of movement. The height of these hedges can affect the speed at which one wants to experience the space. Just as water moves more quickly through a taller or narrower channel, so too do people tend to want to experience a pathway lined with taller or more tightly spaced hedges more quickly (Fig. 5.14). A pathway planted with low shrubs or perennials prompts a lesser feeling of urgency, and while it still defines the edge of the pathway or trail, one tends to want to experience it more slowly. A pathway that curves behind a hedge creates a sense of intrigue and anticipation, inspiring one to explore what is ahead (Fig. 5.15).

Other visual tricks that can be played with hedges and screens include forced perspective and borrowed scenery. Forced perspective can be achieved by planting lines of shrubs not perfectly parallel to one another but slightly converging at a terminal point; this gives the illusion of greater distance, similar to the way lines in a perspective drawing are converged in order to create the illusion of dimension (Fig. 5.16). Similarly, the tops of the hedges may be clipped at a slight downward slant, which also gives the illusion of greater distance. Both of these visual tricks were used extensively in Baroque design and are highly maintenance intensive in order to retain the effect. Borrowed scenery is another way to give the illusion of spaciousness, a technique that has been used for centuries in

5.14 Tall, tightly spaced hedges tend to encourage people to pass through more quickly.

5.15 Low hedges and curved pathways slow movement and create intrigue.

Japanese landscape design. Hedges or other masses of screening plants are arranged in order to block neighboring buildings or property lines and direct views to vistas beyond, giving the illusion that the foreground is more secluded while the landscape and view are more far-reaching (Fig. 5.17).

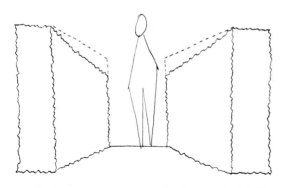

5.16 Hedges that create converging lines manipulate the sense of space in the landscape.

The decorative use of hedges to create parterre gardens or knot gardens has enjoyed popularity at various times in landscape design history, developed during the sixteenth century in France and popularized again during the Victorian era in England, although earlier variations of this style had

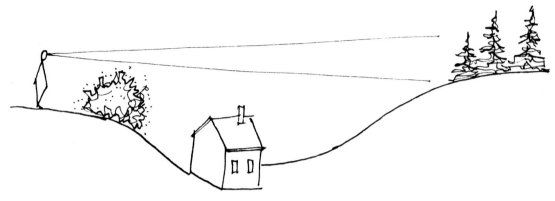

5.17 By blocking buildings and blurring property lines, plants can give the illusion that the landscape is more far-reaching than it really is.

been practiced during medieval times. Parterres and knot gardens are formal arrangements of tightly clipped, very low hedges in geometric patterns, sometimes with colorful plantings or stones in the open spaces between them (Fig. 5.18). Such gardens are meant to resemble embroidery from above. In very formal gardens, low hedges are often planted in complex patterns and forms that must be meticulously maintained. The outer perimeter of such a garden is usually a simple geometric shape, such as a rectangle, a square, or sometimes a circle, with the interior lines creating more complex geometric shapes. The voids between the hedges are then planted with colorful annuals, perennials, or shrubs, or sometimes filled with colorful stones.

We have looked at how plants' specific morphologic characteristics can be used both aesthetically and functionally as design features, but designers can also take cues from the natural world on a more abstract level. Let's take a look in the next chapter.

5.18 Knot garden. (Photo by Adam W. Turner.)

# 6

## CUES FROM NATURE: PLANTS AS DESIGN INSPIRATION

Plants have provided design inspiration for centuries, as architects, designers, and artists in various media have looked to the forms, patterns, and proportions found in nature to assist in composition and design. This chapter focuses on the ways in which the natural proportions of the golden ratio, symmetry, and asymmetry can inform design.

## THE GOLDEN RATIO

During the fifteenth century, architects and designers became much more focused on the impact of the natural world on the sense of order and aesthetics in design. In particular, they were captivated by a repeating ratio that occurs in nature. During the Renaissance, Leonardo da Vinci and Michelangelo, among others, brought order to design by utilizing the golden ratio, or the proportion consis-

tently found in nature that is thought to be the most aesthetically pleasing.

As early as Egyptian times, artists and architects have understood this ratio to be the most pleasing to the eye. In fact, there has been documented a human cognitive preference for the golden section proportions throughout human history. We see the golden ratio demonstrated in the design of everyday objects such as playing cards, writing pads, and books, as well as in great works of art such as the Parthenon, the Great Pyramids, Japanese pagodas, cathedrals throughout the world, the Venus de Milo, *The Birth of Venus* (Botticelli), the *Mona Lisa* (da Vinci), and the *Sistine Madonna* (Raphael)—the list goes on and on. Stonehenge is one of the earliest displays of the golden ratio; the Pentagon in Washington, DC, is one of the more recent.

In essence, a space is considered to

reflect the golden ratio if the ratio of its length to its width approaches 1.618 (for example, a rectangular space of roughly 16' by 10'. This "divine proportion" is based on the mathematics of the Fibonacci sequence, an infinite series of numbers that begins: 0, 1, 1, 2, 3, 5, 8, 13, 21, 34, 55, 89, 144; the first two numbers, by definition, are 0 and 1, and each succeeding number is the sum of the previous two. The golden ratio is the ratio of any two successive numbers in the sequence, for example 144/89, which always approaches 1.618.

The reason the golden ratio is believed to be so aesthetically pleasing is that it is exhibited consistently in nature in the dimensions and proportions of nearly all living creatures, including in the proportions of the human body. For example, a person's height is approximately 1.6 times the length of the torso, the length of face from chin to eyes is approximately 1.6 times the overall length. Because of this relationship to the human form, the ratio tends to be the most comfortable to the human eye and psyche.

There are biological reasons why the golden ratio exists in nature (Posamentier and Lehmann, 2007; Fig. 6.1). For example, each pinecone has two distinct direction spirals, each a Fibonacci number: usually there are 8 spirals in the clockwise direction and 13 in the counterclockwise (Fig. 6.2). This arrangement forms an optimal packing of seeds, so that no matter how large the seed, when they are all identical in size they are efficiently and uniformly packed, with no crowding in the center and no waste of space

6.1 In sunflowers, the spiral arrangement means seeds are packed efficiently.

6.2 Pinecones generally have 8 spirals in the clockwise direction and 13 in the counterclockwise.

at the edge. The hexagonal bracts on a pineapple have a similar quality in the efficiency of their design (Fig. 6.3). These bracts form three different direction spirals, each in 5, 8, and 13 revolutions, all Fibonacci numbers. Among the many plants with spiral arrangements are the daisy, cactus, and sunflower. Of plants displaying spiral arrangements, 92% have a Fibonacci arrangement. Likewise, most flowering plants have petals in a Fibonacci number: the lily and iris have 3, rugosa rose, strawberry, columbine,

6.3 The bracts of a pineapple also present Fibonacci numbers. (Photo by Adam W. Turner.)

6.4 The number of petals of a daisy is often a Fibonacci number.

ber of rotations and the number of leaves to be Fibonacci numbers. Biologically, these arrangements provide the plant with the most efficient means of capturing sunlight and utilizing space.

## SUBDIVISION OF SPACE

From a designer's standpoint, the golden ratio can be very useful, with many practical applications. In fact, artists and designers of nearly every medium—from architects, furniture designers, and garden designers to painters, sculptors, and web designers, and even musicians and poets—have used the golden ratio to help order space and inspire composition. In architecture and interior design, for example, the golden ratio can help determine the dimensions of rooms and placement of furniture, as well as the number and spacing of architectural features such as columns and windows.

In landscape design, a common challenge is the creation of intimate space—space that feels accessible and inviting within a vast open area. One way to accomplish this is by using the rule of the golden ratio to subdivide the landscape into more manageable sections. For example, a multiacre estate or park can be subdivided into smaller gardens, courtyards, or congregation areas that fit within the proportions of the golden ratio, such as an oval lawn area of roughly 50' x 81' or a rectangular courtyard of 45' x 72'. These areas, when sited close to buildings, can feel like an extension of interior space, as their proportions are similar to those of indoor rooms (Fig. 6.5).

pinks, hibiscus, and buttercup have 5, delphinium has 8, marigold has 13, aster has 21, and daisy has either 34, 55, or 89 (Fig. 6.4). We can also find the Fibonacci numbers expressed in the leaves of many plants. If we study the rotations of leaves around the stem of a plant, beginning with the bottom leaf and counting the number of rotations around the stem, each time counting the leaves passed through until reaching the next leaf that is pointing in the same direction as the first, we will find both the num-

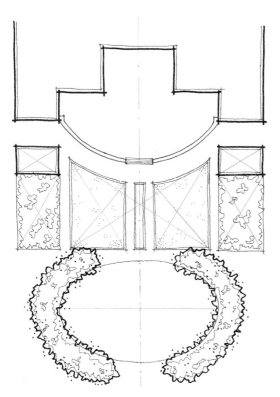

6.5 Spaces that are subdivided based on the golden ratio often have more comfortable proportions.

## PLACEMENT OF VERTICAL ELEMENTS

Outdoor spaces are typically populated with elements that further subdivide them both physically and visually into areas of interest. Vertical elements, such as trees and upright shrubs, can imply enclosure while also creating rhythm and interest in the landscape. When these elements are arranged based on the golden ratio, they can create pleasing compositions. For example, 50' fastigiate trees may be spaced 31' on center to create a vertical, open rectangle based on the golden section. We can also consider the height and placement of the canopy based on the overall height of the tree. For example, a 20' ornamental tree with a canopy that begins around 7.5' can provide a pleasing composition and focus in the landscape. Similarly, the heights and arrangements of plantings can be based on the golden ratio. For example, a planting bed may contain tall, 6.5' screening plants in front of which 4' tall shrubs and 2.5' tall perennials are placed. Each line of plantings subdivides the vertical space based on the

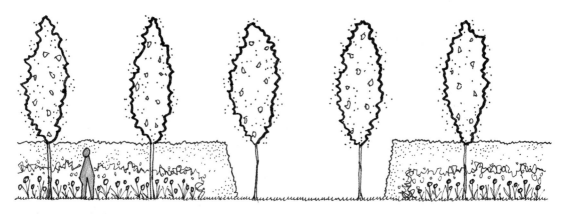

6.6 Elements in the landscape can be placed based on the golden ratio to create interest.

golden section. These vertical proportions provide visually pleasing height contrasts as well as scale in the landscape (Fig. 6.6).

## GROUPING OF PLANTS

Designers often group plants in odd numbers. Elements massed in groups of 3's and 5's are fairly common, as are single specimen plantings. However, we also find that groupings of 2 and 8 can lend a certain feeling of balance, especially when mixed with a proportionate number of "odds." Designers should consider the Fibonacci sequence in plant groupings and quantity specifications.

## PLACEMENT OF COLOR AND FOCAL POINTS

The placement of color at regular intervals within planting beds can also be based on the golden ratio in order to provide rhythm, emphasis, and interest in the landscape. For example, a massing of contrasting color may be placed 18' down a 30' perennial border in order to visually divide and help balance the space. Similarly, a specimen planting or other focal point can also be placed along a bed length or within a lawn area based on the golden ratio.

## SYMMETRY AND ASYMMETRY

The above examples illustrate ways that the golden proportion found in nature can be used in design. But plants' various forms and

patterns can also be used to inspire design, without complicated mathematics. (For more about drawing on natural forms to inspire your design approaches, see the section "Bio-mimicry" in Chapter 10.) Plants provide tremendous variety in color, form, contrast, and pattern. The sculptural Japanese maple, with its twisting branches and irregular branching habit, shows great regularity in the details of its leaves (Figs. 6.7, 6.8). The conical form

6.7, 6.8 The sculptural Japanese maple is irregular from afar (top) but quite regular close up in the pattern of its leaves (bottom). (Bottom photo by Adam W. Turner.)

of the Norway spruce on the other hand, becomes much more random in appearance as we experience it close up. The symmetrical and asymmetrical forms we see in plants have botanical reasons for being. The spruce, for example, is shaped to shed heavy snow and prevent branch breakage in winter, while the Japanese maple has an irregular branching habit to capture the most sunlight and respond to windy conditions. Both patterns of growth, symmetrical and asymmetrical, allow the plant to efficiently capture sunlight, remain structurally stable, and survive its specific environmental conditions. The beautiful forms these create, however, provide us with an appreciation of symmetry and asymmetry that can inspire design.

We can use these patterns to help structure our designed spaces. Formal design tends to employ more symmetry than does informal, often incorporating geometric shapes that are mirrored along a main axis, in much the same way that a leaf has a mirrored pattern along its midrib (Fig. 6.9). These schemes tend to utilize strong linearity, tight forms, and clipped plantings, all which help draw the eye through the landscape and provide a sense of control. Informal design is generally much more asymmetrical and relaxed, with more curves and fewer straight lines (Fig. 6.10). Although we usually refer to informal design as "naturalistic," the symmetry of formal design also takes its inspiration from the natural world.

6.9 An example of formal/symmetrical design.

6.10 An example of informal/asymmetrical design.

These stylistic choices often reflect the nature of the space. For example, a formal landscape can complement a more formal or symmetrical architectural style, such as French Provincial and Italianate, while an informal landscape may be better suited to asymmetrical or informal architecture, such as Tudor or Craftsman, or to spaces meant to look more like native habitats. Proximity to a building can also play a part in style selection: formal landscapes tend to be used near buildings, the style becoming increasingly informal as one moves further away, especially when the site is surrounded by a natural area. But

no matter what the style, balance is the key to a successful space. Balance is achieved in formal design by creating replicas of design elements along a central axis, but it can also be achieved in asymmetrical schemes by establishing a sense of hierarchy among colors, textures, and heights from one area of the design to another without identical repetition.

Plant selection can also play a role in formal and informal design. Because formal designs tend to invoke a feeling of control, dwarf and low-growing plants are often selected, as well as those that have tighter inflorescences and forms or are tolerant of heavy pruning, such as *Buxus*, *Thuja*, *Carpinus*, and *Rosa*. Plants that have a looser form or more whimsical appearance can be better choices for informal design and include such diverse choices as *Gaura lindheimeri*, ornamental grasses, and *Acer palmatum*.

Style of landscape design is a matter of personal preference, influenced by historical trends. From the Middle Ages through the Renaissance, landscapes and gardens were designed as very formal, symmetrical spaces, but beginning in the eighteenth and nineteenth centuries, artists, architects, and designers began a revolt of sorts against the more ornate and so-called artificial aesthetic of the times, inspiring enthusiasm for replicating the natural world. This aesthetic of realism is one that Chinese and Japanese cultures have always embraced. In fact, until recently, design precepts in Chinese and Japanese cultures had not changed much over many centuries, amd were based on an appreciation of nature, simplicity, and restraint, with a tendency toward the more random patterns that exist in nature. Although the style is asymmetrical, it is controlled, with precise placement of elements (Fig. 6.11). These "informal" aesthetic values became even more popular in the nineteenth and twentieth centuries, and during the period of Art Nouveau, where the organic, curvilinear forms of nature populate nearly every designed space, including that of buildings and furniture. In the informality of the English cottage-style garden, asymmetric forms and kaleidoscopic color combinations suggest a lively exuberance.

Today, there appears to be an appreciation of both formal and informal styles of design, highlighting the need for our study of the space and of our client's preferences from the outset of any project. While style preferences are among the first questions a designer should ask a client, those preferences often change as the design process proceeds. Clients may be quick to declare their taste for either formal or informal style, but are then frequently drawn to a particular aspect of the opposing style. Because nature itself will provide examples of both formality and informality, symmetry and asymmetry, it may be intuitive to incorporate both into each design, depending on the unique needs of the client and the site.

6.11 The Japanese style garden is asymmetrical, yet precise in its placement of elements.

Up to this point, we have examined the myriad ways plant science can inform our planting plans and design decisions—ways in which the forms, patterns, and proportions found in nature can help inspire the design and arrangement of plants and other objects within the landscape. But designers also have responsibilities in the field; we must be sure that the individual plants fit our specifications in terms of overall health and are planted in such a way as to support their growth. The next chapter describes how to select plants in the nursery and install them properly on the site.

# 7

## ON THE JOB: FROM SPECIFICATIONS TO INSTALLATIONS

With an increased understanding of the botany that explains plants' cultural needs and functionality, we can improve our abilities to perform many of the tasks involved in implementing our designs, from specifying plant material and examining nursery stock to supervising planting, transplanting, and pruning, to choosing the best woods for hardscape. The next three chapters offer detailed tips to help designers realize their visions in the landscape.

## SPECIFYING PLANT MATERIAL

Before selecting plants at a nursery or examining them once they have arrived at the job site, designers are responsible for clearly specifying the plants we have selected to achieve our designs. In addition to listing the exact species or cultivar in the sizes or quantities we require, we can also make reference to health and nursery standards. A planting schedule should always include, at a minimum, the plant's scientific and common names, any specified cultivars or varieties, the desired size and method of transplantation (height, caliper, container size, B&B, etc.), and any additional qualifications, such as branching height; single-stemmed, multistemmed (originating from a single root system), or clump form (originating from multiple root systems); the minimum number of canes (shrubs' primary stems that originate from the ground); and preference for whether the plant should be pruned or sheared in the nursery. The more information included in the planting schedule and specifications, the better the chance that the contractor will locate and deliver the appropriate plant material to execute your design.

# EVALUATING MODES OF TRANSPLANTATION

Plants are typically exported from the nursery in one of three ways: bare root, balled and burlapped (B&B), or containerized (Fig. 7.1). Each method has its pros and cons in terms of cost, weight, and size, making some methods more suitable to particular situations than others.

## BARE ROOT

Bare-root plantings have no intact rootball, which means no soil is transported along with the root system of the plant. These types of plants must be transported only while they are dormant, and special care must be taken to prevent dormancy break and root desiccation before they are planted and seasonal conditions are conducive to new growth. Because of the process undertaken to prepare bare root plants (plants are excavated from the ground and the soil is washed clean), few, if any, root tips are left intact. This can make the reestablishment of the plant difficult if proper steps are not taken to encourage new growth of the smaller feeder roots. Bare-root plants tend to be less expensive because they are lighter in weight, since there is no heavy soil around the roots, which reduces transportation and handling costs.

The bare-root method has primarily been used in transplanting small shrubs and trees, though recent studies have also shown success with larger plantings, such as street trees, especially if consistent irrigation is provided

(Anella, Hennessey, and Lorenzi, 2008). This mode of transplantation is also beneficial when multiple small plants are required for a design, such as along a steep slope, because they tend to be cheaper alternatives to B&B or containerized plants.

## BALLED AND BURLAPPED

Balled and burlapped (B&B) plants differ from bare-root plants in that once the plant is excavated from the earth, the soil is left intact. The entire rootball, containing both roots and soil, is wrapped in burlap and transported. Because of the soil, these plants can be quite heavy—much more so than one might suppose—especially after irrigation when the soil becomes saturated. Plans should be made accordingly for proper transport and placement of B&B plants once they have reached the job site.

This method of transplantation is often the preferred method for larger trees and shrubs, as plots of plantings can be left in place at the nursery for several years before plants reach the size required for sale. If executed properly, an initial cut with a sharp spade will be made to the root system somewhere inside the dripline of the canopy. A period of recov-

7.1 Modes of transplantation: bare root, balled & burlapped, and containerized.

ery time is needed in order to encourage the pruned roots to sprout new feeder roots; the plant will then be excavated from the ground and its rootball will be wrapped. Because significant root pruning still occurs with this method, steps should be taken to encourage new root growth once the plant is installed on site, including providing sufficient water and soil nutrition and perhaps adding biostimulants to the soil. This mode of transplantation can be a good choice when larger specimens are desired; however, because of their size and weight, B&B plants tend to be the most expensive type of transplant.

## CONTAINERIZED

Containerized plants are typically grown in a plastic or wooden container of a specific size and can be either transplanted into a larger container or sold at their original size. The benefit of containerized plants is that the small feeder roots and root tips are left intact instead of being removed by excavating from the soil. If plants are grown too long in these containers, however, they begin to form circling roots. Circling roots occur when roots, which normally grow laterally, hit a solid surface such as the container wall and begin growing around the perimeter of the container. This pattern of root growth can continue after the plant is transplanted into the site soil if not corrected at the time of planting and can lead to girdling roots, which can eventually cut off the proper flow of water and nutrients to the plant and cause structural instability. Proper treatment of circling

roots for smaller herbaceous plants includes "teasing" the roots by gently disentangling them and directing them toward outward growth; for larger plants, shrubs, or trees, the outer surface of the rootball may need to be scored with a sharp knife, which prunes the roots and causes new growth to grow laterally. Sometimes containers are treated with a substance containing copper or another root growth inhibitor, which has been shown in some studies to chemically prune the roots and prevent them from circling.

Another problem with containerized plants is the interface between the container soil and the site soil. Often the container soil is better suited to root growth, which can prevent roots from growing outside that medium and into the surrounding soil. Also, the site soil is often more compacted than the container medium, preventing roots from penetrating the interface. Despite these challenges, the benefits of using containerized plants, besides an intact root system, include their lower cost and lighter weight. In most cases, these plants are smaller and more easily transported and handled than B&B plants.

## EXAMINING NURSERY STOCK

Every designer who specifies plant material should have a basic understanding of how to properly select a healthy plant in the nursery. Depending on how a plant is to be used in a design, we may have varying means to evaluate the plant for its artistic value. But, the overall health of the plant is not something to

be compromised. Even if we cannot person-
ally hand-select each plant, when plant material is delivered to the site, we should quickly
be able to determine whether material should
be approved for installation or rejected out-
right. A designer always has the responsibility of accepting or rejecting unhealthy plants,
whether in the nursery or once a shipment
has arrived on site. A keen eye to plant health
will help ensure the long-term viability of the
landscape.

There are several ways to evaluate plant
health by examining both the shoots (the
aboveground portions of the plant) and the
roots (generally the below-ground portion).

## SHOOTS

The shoots are generally the most visually
accessible and therefore the first indicators
of the health and desirability of a plant. We
often look for symmetry (or lack thereof),
density, and branching height of specified
plantings that can enhance our designs and
fulfill particular functional or aesthetic needs
in the landscape (Figs. 7.2, 7.3). Beyond
their artistic characteristics, the shoots can
be indicators of good health. A plant should
have appropriate branching structure (Fig.
7.4). Trees (both deciduous and evergreen)
should have a single, straight, self-supporting
main stem centered within the crown, as
opposed to multiple weak leaders. Branches
off the main leader should have strong attach-
ments, with crotch angles that do not contain
included bark, or bark that forms in tight
crotch angles and can weaken the structural

stability of a tree branch (Fig. 7.5). The trunk
of the tree or canes of a shrub should also be
free of any cracks or cavities. If a protective
covering is present on the trunk, it should be
removed so the bark can be inspected. Be
leery of nurseries that keep trunks wrapped
and tied with fabric or plastic, unless they

7.2 This B&B katsura tree shows good symmetry and
density, both indicators of a healthy plant. (Select Horticulture, Inc., Lancaster, MA; photo by the author.)

7.3 'Matsu' apples trees may be selected based on their
artistic branching and interesting form. (Select Horticulture,
Inc., Lancaster, MA; photo by the author.)

als, including perennials and annuals, should have dense, healthy canopies or foliage, with healthy terminal buds and leaves that are free of signs of drought stress, winter die-back, and discoloration. Leaves should also be free of insect and disease damage and be of normal size for that particular plant at that time of year. Stems should also be free of insect, mechanical, and disease damage. Stems of trees and shrubs, if previously pruned, should show signs of healthy callus tissue. We should also be wary of suckers (vigorous upright shoots) growing from the bases of trees, as they are indicators of plant stress (Fig. 7.6).

7.4 This red maple shows appropriate branching structure, with a straight trunk and strong, evenly spaced lateral branches. (Select Horticulture, Inc., Lancaster, MA; photo by the author.)

## ROOTS

When examining plants in the nursery, we should not neglect the rootball, which can

7.5 Plant material should have wide crotch angles with no included bark.

have just been delivered to the nursery or are about to be shipped to a site, as the wrappings invite a host of pests and diseases and hide blemishes that signify an unhealthy plant. The main branches of the tree or canes of a shrub should be uniform and evenly distributed around the center of the plant and show signs of appropriate shoot elongation.

Trees, shrubs, and herbaceous materi-

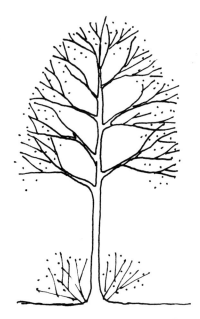

7.6 Avoid selecting plants with suckers growing from the rootball.

easily be overlooked since it is mostly hidden from view. I have often climbed into the middle of a block of trees at a nursery in order to untie and inspect the crown and roots of B&B trees. We should not be deterred from untying burlap or lifting rootballs out of containers in order to assess the health of the root system. Roots should be made up only of healthy tissue that is light in color and not dried out, damaged, malodorous, or diseased in any way. Roots should fill the rootballs evenly around the base of the main stem, but not be so dense as to be completely pot-bound or growing profusely out of drain holes (Fig. 7.7). Likewise, the soil mix within a container should be within 2" of the top. We should also note where the plant's root flare, or crown (the area where the roots meet the stem), is located in relation to the soil level; root flares should never be covered with soil when planted on site, so if harvesting methods have caused flares

to be covered for transport, they should be identified and uncovered prior to planting.

Other markers that can assist in healthy plant selection include whether or not weeds are growing out of the container or burlap, how secure the plant is within the rootball (it should feel firm when shaken), and whether the main stem is centered within the container or rootball. The size of the rootball should also be noted. The American Nursery and Landscape Association (formerly the American Association of Nurserymen) has developed appropriate, industry-accepted standards for nursery stock (see the 2004 edition, *American Standard for Nursery Stock*). Their guidelines include standardized sizes, the proper relationship between height and caliper (diameter of trunk) or height and width of plants, and where to measure them, and appropriate materials and application methods for B&B. Designers who specify plant material should become familiar with these standards for nursery stock and make reference to them where appropriate.

7.7 Pot-bound plants often have roots growing out of the drainage holes.

## SUPERVISING PLANTING AND TRANSPLANTING

While planting techniques are generally the responsibility of the contractor, who needs to uphold any warranty agreements, it is good practice for designers to have a general knowledge of proper planting techniques as well (Figs. 7.8, 7.9). An educated designer can identify problems in the field during construction as well as provide site-specific installation details that will assist in the longevity of the plantings. These details should identify, at a minimum, planting adjustments based on specific soil conditions (such as tilling compacted soil and modifying planting heights based on drainage patterns) and seasonal timelines for planting.

Transplanting is an unnatural process. As much as 90% of the root system of a plant can be lost in the process of harvesting and transport. Therefore, proper treatment of the root system is critical to reestablishment, which can take many years, regardless of the amount of care given.

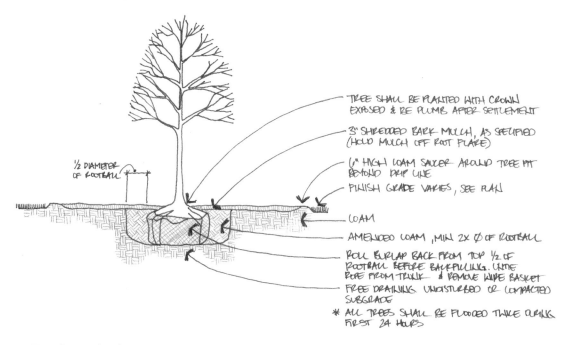

7.8 Tree planting detail.

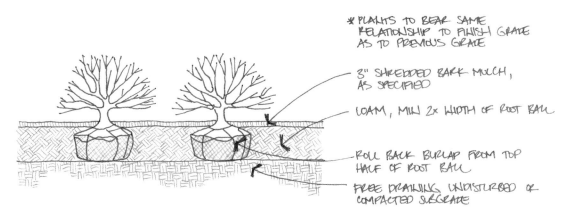

7.9 Shrub planting detail.

## PROPER TRANSPLANTING TECHNIQUES

A successful transplant involved four basic steps:

### Step 1: Digging the hole

For trees and large shrubs, as a general rule, the bottom of the rootball should sit on undisturbed soil that is excavated to a depth that places the plant in the same relationship to the finished grade as it was prior to being harvested. With perennials and annuals, the soil below the plant should not be as compact and undisturbed, as the weight of the plant is not an issue. Bulbs are an exception to this rule of planting at grade; they should be planted to a depth of approximately 3 times their width. This at-grade rule may also be broken if site soil conditions are not conducive to good drainage, in which case we may want to specify that rootballs be planted slightly high (up to a few inches) in order to prevent poor aeration. The crown of a plant, or its root flare, should not under any circumstances be buried. While planting holes for trees and shrubs should be dug no deeper than the depth of the rootball, they should be dug approximately 3 times the width (or as much as the situation will allow, but not less than ⅓ greater than the diameter of the rootball), ensuring that roots have ample volume of uncompacted soil in order to grow laterally and begin to reestablish. Perennials and annuals also benefit from the digging of large enough holes to allow roots to spread into friable soil without obstruction.

### Step 2: Preparing the plant

Prior to planting, all plant materials should be protected from harsh sun and winds and should not be allowed to dry out. This may mean spraying plants with an antidessicant or keeping them in their containers in the shade and maintaining appropriate irrigation. Once planting commences, a common mistake, particularly with trees and shrubs, is the failure to remove the burlap, wires, tags, or cages from the plant. When B&B plants are set into the ground, all burlap should be removed from the side of the rootball; if the bottom piece of burlap is left in place, it should not be clumped together, but rather spread out as much as possible. Even though nursery standards require burlap to be biodegradable, studies have shown that the length of time needed for the material to biodegrade can impede lateral growth of roots and lengthen the time for reestablishment. Likewise, the cages that help secure the burlap and rootballs should always be removed with wire cutters, as these wires have been shown to girdle roots as root diameters increase with maturity. Similarly, tags (both plastic and metal) and staking wires can girdle stems and trunks if they are left on for too long.

Before plants are removed from their containers, they should be groomed by removing yellowed or browned foliage, pruning broken branches or stems, and deadheading spent blooms. Once the plant is removed from the container, its root system can be examined to ensure that all roots are alive and healthy and facing in an outward direction; if this is not the case, prune dead or damaged root tissue, and score or coax circling roots outward to encourage their lateral growth into the soil of the planting bed.

## Step 3: Backfilling

Once the hole is dug and the plant is set at the proper level and stripped of any impeding materials, soil can be backfilled to secure the plant in place. For trees and large shrubs, backfill should be applied in layers no greater than 8", tamping after each layer before the next layer is placed; when the hole is ⅔ filled, it should be thoroughly watered before applying the remainder of the backfill in order to eliminate any air pockets and ensure good contact between roots and soil. Roots should be encouraged to grow beyond the hole and into site soil as soon as possible. For containerized plants—annuals, perennials, and small shrubs—tamp the backfill lightly once all soil is in place, again, in order to eliminate air pockets.

In recent years, there has been much debate over whether amendments, such as compost or peat moss, should be added to backfill soil or whether 100% native soil is the best choice. The argument lies in the interface between amended soil and site soil and whether it will deter plant roots from crossing over that interface. To date, reports from field experiments have been conflicting; however, amendments, if they are used, should only comprise a small percentage (less than ⅓) of the backfill soil. Native soil (or the same soil that has been established throughout the site or planting bed) should usually make up the majority of the backfill.

One amendment that has received some attention in recent years is mycorrhizae, a fungus that forms a symbiotic (mutually beneficial) association with the roots of many plants. The fungus colonizes the roots of plants either intracellularly (entering into plant cells) or extracellularly (not entering into plant cells) in order to obtain sugars, or food energy. The benefit to the plant is that it extends and greatly increases the surface area of the root system to assist the plant in the uptake of water and nutrients, making this amendment especially beneficial in nutrient-poor soils. Mycorrhizal inoculations can now be purchased and added to planting soil to potentially increase the health and establishment of plants, especially in nutrient-poor, drought-susceptible, or otherwise infertile soils.

## Step 4: Staking, mulching, and watering

Mulch should be applied immediately after planting and watering. A covering of mulch should be spread over planting beds in order to prevent weed cover, increase organic matter content of the soil, moderate soil temperature, and prevent water loss. Mulch should not be applied any thicker than 3" deep around trees and shrubs (often less around perennials and annuals), and it should not be applied within 6–8" of trunks of trees and shrubs, nor should it bury the crowns of perennials; if mulch covers a plant's crown, it can trap moisture against the crown and potentially lead to rot and can also attract vermin, which may nest and cause damage. Plants should be thoroughly watered twice within the first 24 hours of installation, and irrigation should be closely monitored until the plants are established. Tree stakes should only be installed if site conditions are conducive to heavy winds that could topple trees; light winds have been shown to be beneficial in promoting greater trunk girth and structural stability. If tree stakes are deemed necessary, they should always be removed after one full growing season, once sufficient rooting has been established (Fig. 7.10).

Specifying plants, examining nursery stock, and understanding proper planting techniques will help us write detailed planting specifications that not only enhance our designs but also promote healthy, enduring landscapes, with plants with vigorous root systems. But we must also be aware of the challenges these roots can present in the landscape, understand how site conditions can promote problems, and take appropriate steps to avoid or remedy these problems.

## CHALLENGES WITH ROOTS

Designers are typically focused on the aesthetic and spatial characteristics of a plant— those that can be seen, smelled, or otherwise experienced in space, above ground level. But the hidden, underground roots deserve just as much attention from the standpoints of safety, plant health, and maintenance as do all the other design features mentioned in previous chapters. Roots anchor plants in the ground and are responsible for absorbing and transporting the water and minerals crucial to their survival. The root system of a plant can be extensive; although generally existing in the top 6" of the soil profile, roots occupy a space that can be 10–20% wider than a plant's canopy (or much greater for large trees). Thus, it is not surprising that many landscape problems begin below ground, within the soil.

Roots can grow in many patterns below ground. Some plants, such as *Juniperus* and *Physocarpus*, have root systems that are much more finely branched and fibrous than others, spreading out to find water, nutrients, and space. Other plants, such as young *Quercus* and *Pseudotsuga*, have a main root (taproot) with few side branches, growing more deeply into the earth. Still others form adventitious roots, or roots off their stems, which help them to colonize and spread over the surface of the earth, as do *Hedera helix* and *Campsis radicans*. As a general rule, the

7.10 Tree stakes should be installed if conditions warrant them, and should be removed after one season.

finer roots that occur at the outer reaches of the root system are the feeder roots, which are not only most active in absorbing water and nutrients but are also most susceptible to damage during transplant, construction, and compaction. Older roots are those that occur closer to the crown of the plant (the junction between the root and stem) and tend to be thicker and more structural in nature.

Because of the extent of the root systems of plants, it is crucial that planting beds provide adequate soil volume. Most moderately sized street trees require 300–400 cubic feet of soil without the presence of irrigation. Unfortunately, most urban street tree plantings only receive about 48 cubic feet (4' x 4' x 3') due to the presence of concrete footings and foundations, sidewalks, roadways, and underground utilities (Fig. 7.11). Shrubs and herbaceous plantings such as annuals and perennials also fall victim to lack of soil, especially in planters or raised beds that are too small for their root systems. The soil that is available must be able to provide the plant with the water and nutrients it needs, and even then the roots will still try to extend beyond that, seeking more space and resources and potentially causing problems in the landscape.

## PAVEMENT

Roots are opportunistic, constantly seeking out resources needed to survive. If plants, especially trees, sense additional resources under pavement or along foundations or curbing, their roots will grow toward these areas and may cause damage, particularly if the trees are more established (greater than 8" trunk diameter; Fig. 7.12). Soil immediately beneath sidewalk and road pavements usually has a higher moisture content than the trees' miniscule planting pits. These pavements are prone to swings in temperature, which rises during the day due to solar radiation and then cools drastically at night, creating condensation that cannot evaporate because of the solid surface above it. This trapped water is more available to the roots that seek it out, eventually causing heaving and cracking in the pavement above.

7.11 Urban street trees rarely get the soil volume they need for healthy growth.

7.12 Roots that seek out resources can wreak havoc on pavements.

Fortunately, several strategies have proved somewhat successful in preventing damage by tree roots, including the use of root barriers, exclusion zones, flexible pavements, and structural soils.

- **Root barriers** of various types appear to be the most successful in preventing pavement damage (Fig. 7.13). Some act as traps, comprising a wire or fabric mesh that allows only the smallest feeder roots to pass through; these small roots are not capable of damaging pavements. Other barriers act as deflectors, changing root direction; these are made of fabric or plastic and can be installed either in a linear configuration, creating a wall between the tree roots and the pavement, or encircling the trunk. Because encircling barriers may encourage roots to grow in a circular pattern, which can eventually create girdling and prevent movement of water and nutrients, "ribs" are formed in the wall of the barrier or chemical inhibitors are coated on the wall's surface in order to direct root growth downward. In these instances, the barrier should be no deeper than 12" so roots can exit below. In addition, barriers should be installed to penetrate the surface of the soil and should not be covered over with mulch, or else the roots will eventually find their way over them.

- **Exclusion zones** are areas of physical or chemical change in soils that prevent root growth in much the same way as do root barriers. Instead of plastic or fabric, a trench of soil that is mechanically

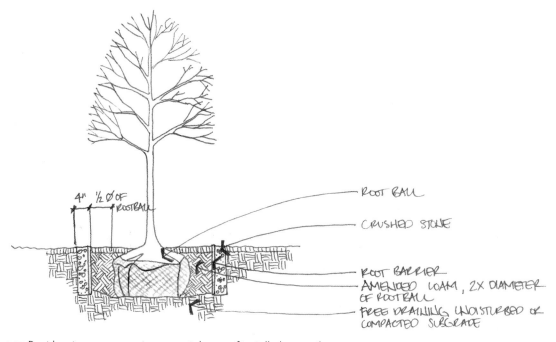

7.13 Root barriers can prevent pavement damage if installed correctly.

or chemically altered by compacting or injecting with clay slurry or concrete solution is installed around the planting area to deter roots from extending beyond. Alternately, air gaps can be utilized to create exclusion zones. Large pieces of stone (including, often, construction debris) are installed in the soil trench; the stones' very large pores prevent water from being held. These stone matrices dry out quickly and deter roots from growing into them. Finally, and most severely, "kill zones" are areas in which the portions of a root system that are in too close contact with a structure are removed; this is accomplished either by mechanical pruning of the roots with tools or equipment or by destroying portions of the roots with chemicals. This last practice is not widely recommended, as it leaves plants susceptible to pathogens and structural instability.

- **Flexible pavements** represent another series of new technologies that are also providing solutions to the root versus pavement problem. One such example is Rubbersidewalks, a recycled rubber modular sidewalk paving system invented by a public works inspector from Santa Monica, California, to solve the problem of sidewalk damage from tree roots. The 100% recycled crumb rubber from waste tires is combined with a polyurethane binder and colorant and then molded under heat and pressure into high-density modular paving tiles. Individual tiles can be removed and replaced, and thus

roots can be trimmed. Flexi-pave is a product made of similar materials, but it is cast-in-place as opposed to modular (Fig. 7.14). It is not only flexible but also highly pervious to stormwater, reducing the need for stormwater retention. Each of these systems is strong enough to withstand pedestrian traffic (walkers, runners, skateboarders, rollerbladers, and bicyclists) as well as low-speed or lightweight vehicles, such as cars in parking lots or golf carts; both are skid resistant and reduce fall injury because of their impact-absorbing qualities. These products come in a wide array of colors, and while initial costs can be up to a third higher than traditional pavement, it is expected that long-term maintenance and liability costs will be much lower. Forthcoming studies will tell us for sure.

While there has been some recent concern about the environmental impact of recycled rubber products on the envi-

7.14 This highly flexible cast-in-place product created from recycled rubber tires prevents damage from tree roots and reduces stormwater runoff (KBI Flexi®-pave). (Photo by Christopher S. Chapin.)

ronment (from toxic leachate, dust, etc.), several studies have shown little to no environmental impact on drinking water, waterways, or plants—levels were not high enough to trigger EPA guidelines (Humphrey and Swett 2006; Sullivan 2006). It has been noted, however, that longer-range effects are still unknown, and that leachate may be affected by local soil and water pH. The two products mentioned above use a polyurethane binder, which encapsulates the rubber and apparently prevents particles from escaping. But the polyurethane initially releases volatile organic compounds (VOCs) that can pose an environmental hazard. In considering the use of any such alternative products, we must educate ourselves and weigh the risks against the benefits in order to promote sustainability of our designed landscapes.

- **Structural soil** is created using a similar method to that of exclusion zones, but instead of injecting the voids between the crushed stone with clay slurry or concrete to deter root growth, the large pores are filled with a clay loam to support plant life. The product, called CU-Soil, was developed at the Urban Horticulture Institute at Cornell University, and is composed of large, angular, crushed stone mixed with a clay loam soil. The mixture is held together with a nontoxic hydrogel tackifier and supports the structural requirements of landscape installations as well as the biological requirements of plants. CU-soil, which has been used in New York City, Cincinnati, Ohio, and Cambridge, Massachusetts, has shown great promise in supporting urban street tree growth while impeding pavement heaving.

## TURF

Tree roots may also cause landscape problems when they compete with the roots of turf or other groundcover planted beneath them. The roots of all plants seek out water and nutrients; if different types of plants are in close proximity, they will compete for these resources. When trees are underplanted with turf, groundcover, or low perennials and ample resources are not available, one or the other may struggle. One way to prevent this is to create a ring of mulch at the base of the tree that is at a minimum the diameter of the tree's rootball and at a maximum the diameter of its canopy (Fig. 7.15). This ring of mulch should be increased in size as the canopy size increases. Mulch, while eliminat-

7.15 Mulch beneath trees should extend to the canopy line whenever possible.

ing competition between roots, also provides the soil with increased organic matter and decreases water loss. Another solution is to specify appropriate plant combinations that can survive in these microclimates created by plant competition. For example, *Epimedium*, *Liriope*, *Pachysandra*, and many *Hemerocallis* varieties can grow well in the dry shade that exists beneath trees.

## UNDERGROUND UTILITIES

Although a less frequent problem than heaving of pavement, roots can sometimes invade and plug storm drains or other underground pipes, especially if these pipes have been structurally compromised and are cracked. Older clay and concrete pipes with gasket connections tend to be more prone to damage than newer plastic pipes, as these pipes usually have more cracks and are easier to penetrate. Roots often seek out pipes for two reasons: first, if the soils around the pipes are compacted or poorly draining, the roots will grow toward these areas of greater oxygen content; and second, if the roots do not have sufficient space in their planting medium, they will penetrate pipe cracks in order to access more space.

## ROOM TO EXPAND

Roots seek space to expand and grow in order to provide their ever-enlarging shoot system with both increased water and nutrients and the additional structural support needed to stand upright. For example, the larger and heavier the canopy of a tree, the more the roots must expand and anchor themselves in the earth. If the soil saturated, either from heavy rainfall or poor drainage, and a sudden or sustained gust of high wind occurs, the tree is likely to topple and cause damage to neighboring structures or harm to passersby. Therefore, creating a broader area for rooting, especially for large trees, is imperative.

Many of the problems that are blamed on trees and other plantings are often the result of design and engineering failures and can therefore be prevented. Poorly designed pipes, inadequate design of pavement, poor species selection, and improper location of plantings cause a host of maintenance and liability problems. We know that roots are opportunistic, carefully assessing soil conditions and seeking out the resources they need in order to survive. With our improved understanding of these needs, and where in the landscape they might be met, we can fairly easily predict where roots will grow, and thus help prevent unnecessary, costly, or dangerous maintenance and liability issues down the road. We can also take greater control of root growth by providing more favorable conditions for roots away from structures, by creating broader swaths of resource-rich soils to keep roots in check, and by selecting site-appropriate plant species. We can also be more vigilant in insuring that pavement sub-bases are designed and installed correctly, that damage to pavements is not caused by frost or water issues unrelated to plants, and that root barriers are specified as needed (Fig. 7.16).

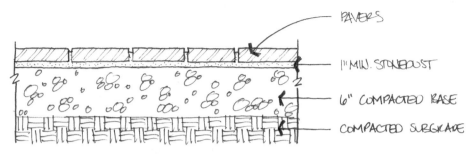

PAVERS

1" MIN. STONEDUST

6" COMPACTED BASE

COMPACTED SUBGRADE

7.16 Sub-bases should be designed and installed correctly to prevent pavement failure.

Proper specification, examination, and installation of nursery stock, as well as specification of techniques to prevent common landscape problems, are the first steps to a successful designed landscape, but we must also be sure our design intent will remain intact after we leave the job site. The long-term success of our projects hinges on the establishment of comprehensive maintenance plans that give detailed instructions on how to care for the landscape as it ages.

## MAINTENANCE PLANS

It is imperative for designers to take an active role in the maintenance plan of a landscape. Recommendations for caring for the elements of the design should always be provided from the outset in order to ensure that a landscape matures successfully and maintains the designer's intent. We should have an understanding of the level of maintenance our clients intend in terms of time, budget, and resources and design to those standards.

That level may vary greatly from client to client. A commercial landscape with few resources for maintenance, for example, probably does not warrant a garden filled with hybrid tea roses or formally pruned hedges that require hours of care. Hardier, lower-maintenance shrubs such as *Rosa rugosa*, *Spiraea*, or *Weigela* might be better choices. Conversely, a large estate with extensive gardens may require and allow a much higher level of care. I had the privilege of walking the grounds of a renovated oceanfront estate in Bar Harbor, Maine, with both the landscape architect and the estate's gardener. The two exhibited a close working relationship, as the landscape architect talked in great detail about how he restored the "bones" of the site, recapturing the original symmetry and formality of the gardens, and the gardener talked at length about continuously experimenting with new cultivars of annuals and perennials and adjusting the watering and pruning regimens to maintain the design scheme and provide seasonal interest. Each professional's skill set contributed to the ongoing success of the landscape, but in very different ways: the landscape architect was respectful of the gardener's knowledge about plantings and new introductions that could highlight the features of the garden, while the gardener was mindful of maintaining the overall intent of the geometries, balance, and movement of the space.

Regardless of the level of anticipated care, it is important to communicate to our clients that no landscape is free of maintenance needs. Some plantings need less pruning or watering, less weeding or deadheading, and requirements may change as the landscape ages, but a basic level of ongoing maintenance is always needed in order to preserve the health of the landscape and the spirit of the design. Most public projects should specify a skilled professional gardener/horticulturist as a member of the maintenance team. For private projects, the source of these skills may vary, from a knowledgeable homeowner to a trained landscape contractor or highly skilled estate gardener. In many situations, however, we may need to encourage our clients to hire someone with sufficient horticultural knowledge to execute maintenance tasks in such a way as to preserve the health and vigor of the landscape, and we should provide a detailed maintenance plan to ensure our design intent is preserved.

The following section outlines the basic topics to address in a maintenance plan.

## SOIL

Healthy soils are of the utmost importance to the overall vigor of a plant and the reason why soil tests should be conducted every few years, or more frequently if problems arise. In order for soils to continue to provide plant-ings with the nutrients, water, and air they require, they must contain appropriate levels of organic matter, pH, and pore space. Organic matter can be incorporated into the soil either by topdressing with compost or by allowing leaf litter to decompose within plant beds. Soil pH can be adjusted as necessary with the addition of sulfur or lime products, based on the recommendations of soil tests. Biostimulants may also be applied in lieu of, or in combination with, adjusting pH in order to aid plants in extracting nutrients.

In addition, soil compaction should be monitored regularly. Compaction is one of plants' worst enemies, degrading pore space and reducing the amount of available water and air to root systems, thereby causing plants stress and susceptibility to attack by insects and pathogens. Designers can conduct post-occupancy evaluations—analyses conducted after a site has been occupied for some length of time—in order to identify any new or previously undetected pedestrian pathways that appear within turf areas or plant beds. These can be reduced or eliminated by installing deterrents or creating new routes that redirect traffic away from sensitive roots. As another means of amelioration, soil aeration can be performed, especially within turf areas, although it is often more difficult to remediate the problem after compaction has occurred.

## IRRIGATION

Designers should recommend periodic testing of irrigation systems, with an eye to water conservation and preventive equipment maintenance, and specify irrigation routines that are responsive to changes in plant requirements, weather patterns, and microclimates. Once plants are established, they generally require an average of 1" of water per week over the course of 2–3 irrigation sessions, in order to promote deep rooting. Irrigation systems should have an operable rain gauge that reduces their use during rainy periods, as well as a timer that turns systems on in the early morning, allowing leaves to dry in the sunlight and preventing fungal disease. Irrigation should be reduced or eliminated in the late fall in order to promote plants' hardening off in preparation for winter dormancy.

## DEADHEADING, DIVIDING, AND WEEDING

Deadheading (removing the spent blooms of flowers), while time consuming, is important for some plants, such as annuals and bulbs, which when deadheaded revert energy back to the root system in order to prolong the future potential for blooms. Other plants, such as *Geranium*, *Coreopsis*, and *Rosa*, can even produce multiple flushes of blooms within the same season if they are deadheaded. A third category of plants, those with long stalks, such as *Hemerocallis*, *Hosta*, *Digitalis*, *Iris*, and *Paeonia*, and shrubs with unsightly seedpods, such as *Rhododendron* and *Syringa*, will look "cleaner" if they are deadheaded after blooming, and attention, as well as plant energy, will be directed back to the foliage. But some plants, such as *Viburnum*, *Rosa*, and *Cor-*

*nus*, should not be deadheaded if the fruits, which may attract wildlife or serve as a design feature, are desired. Our ability to visualize plants during each phase of their seasonal life cycles is necessary to our specifying appropriate instructions for deadheading.

Some plants, such as *Hosta*, *Hemerocallis*, and *Iris*, develop an abundant underground root system that allows them to spread horizontally over the earth. These plants should be divided every few years, preferably in the fall, as their groupings increase in size. Dividing requires that large colonies of plantings are broken up into smaller clumps and transplanted to areas where they have more space to grow. If allowed to become overcrowded, plants can start to experience poor flower production as they compete for water and nutrients.

Weeding may be periodically necessary, especially during the first couple of seasons before plants mature and fill any bare spots on the ground. A layer of mulch is often sufficient to prevent weed growth, although mechanical removal may still be necessary from time to time. Some professionals recommend the use of a weed barrier fabric or pre-emergent weed killer, but both should be used with great caution. Weed barrier fabrics can prevent water and air from penetrating to the soil below and can be a terrible headache to remove after the fact. Chemical weed killers can harm adjacent plantings, including those that you may want to reseed themselves, such as *Digitalis*, *Aquilegia*, and *Cosmos*, as they add toxins to the environment.

## MULCHING

Another important consideration in landscape maintenance is the application of mulch. Mulch provides many benefits to plants, including increasing organic matter, reducing water loss, reducing weed growth, moderating soil temperature, reducing soil erosion, and preventing weed whackers and lawn mowers from getting too close to tree trunks. Mulch should consist of bark or other composted or inert organic materials such as buckwheat hulls, cocoa shells, leaf litter, pine needles, newspaper, or wood chips. Mulch should be applied to a depth no greater than 3" and away from the crowns of plants (the region where stem and roots meet). It may be necessary to topdress lightly with a thin layer of mulch every season in order to replenish what has washed away or decomposed, but be sure to specify layers below 3".

## PRUNING

Designers should set forth a pruning schedule that is customized both to the design goals and to the natural habits of the trees and shrubs that have been selected, always with the purpose of promoting the health of the plant. Too many examples exist of poor pruning practices in the landscape, where shrubs are purposelessly sheared into separate yet mismatched globes or trees are "topped" without consideration of their natural form.

The maintenance plan should clearly specify the design intent so that as the landscape matures it continues to capture the designer's vision. The next chapter covers pruning in much more detail, but as a general rule the timing of pruning is very important. Different plants produce flower buds at different times of year; if a plant is not pruned at the appropriate time, its flower buds may be inadvertently removed and the plant will not showcase the design feature for which it was selected. Similarly, plants generally respond to pruning with a flush of new growth, not ideal during hot, dry spells or other times of potential plant stress, such as imminent frost.

## PREVENTING INSECT AND DISEASE PROBLEMS

Plants should be checked periodically throughout the season for insects or disease and treated accordingly. Plants are more susceptible to pests and diseases if they are already stressed, so sources of environmental stress and favorable environments for pests or pathogens should be determined and eliminated. Likewise, if a new insect is introduced into an area, a biological or chemical control can be identified and applied. A good resource for pest and disease control is your local cooperative extension. If a plant does become diseased, prevent spread by cleaning up any plant debris and removing it from the site. Avoid composting or disposing of debris near healthy plants and be sure pruning tools are disinfected between cuts.

## WINTER DAMAGE AND SNOW REMOVAL

Winter temperatures can be a primary concern in some landscapes, especially those at higher elevations and latitudes. Some plants, such as hydrangeas, while generally suited to these colder regions, may experience flower bud damage during times of very low temperatures or prolonged winter winds; a good preventative measure is to tie together the stems of these plants in a bundle and cover them with burlap or mulch in order to provide additional protection, especially during seasons with little snow cover. Broadleaf evergreens, such as rhododendrons, azaleas, and hollies, can also benefit from applications of an antidessicant, which protects leaves with a waxy coating and helps prevents water loss.

Designers in temperate climates that experience persistent winter snow cover should address snow removal in the maintenance plan. Indicate a designated area where plows can mound snow away from tender plantings, and make recommendations for less destructive deicing products, such as calcium chloride, calcium magnesium acetate, or sand. Recommend the installation of temporary winter barriers such as snow fencing or burlap around particularly sensitive plantings. And where plants have declined due to salt damage, replacements should consist of more salt-tolerant plants.

## LAWN CARE

Turf areas often require more maintenance than any other plantings in the landscape, and this should be communicated clearly to the client during the design phase. Mowing, weed prevention, fertilization, and irrigation are tasks that require particular attention in order to keep lawns healthy and thriving. While mowing is important, it is often done incorrectly. Grass benefits from being cut "high" (2½–3" at a minimum) during midsummer dry spells because the foliage protects the soil and root zone from too much water loss. Similarly, mowing heights should be set to remove no greater than ⅓ of the existing grass blade at any given pass. Weed growth, nutrient availability, and irrigation needs are all dependent on soil health; soil tests must be repeated periodically to check for nutrient deficiencies, pH levels, and pore space. Often, soil compaction and deicing salts create a beneficial environment for crabgrass, a very hardy and opportunistic weed. In order to eliminate crabgrass and other turf weeds, environments should be adjusted so turf can thrive; gypsum can be applied in spring to leach salts out of the soil and nutrient levels can be kept at ideal levels for turf growth through the addition of compost and organic matter. Traditional lawn-care programs require regular applications of both fertilizers and pesticides, but in specifying lawn care maintenance, we can look to more recent practices of providing soil nutrition and insect and disease control through organic methods described below.

## FERTILIZATION

The first two or three years after a landscape is installed can be a time of high vulnerability for plants; they undergo extreme stress when they are transplanted as they generally lose a large portion of their root system and need to acclimate to a new environment. The maintenance plan should specify an approach to plant care that ensures sufficient nutrient availability while plants are getting established. This should almost always include the addition of organic matter, primarily in the form of compost, which not only increases the efficiency of nutrient uptake, but also supports beneficial microbial activity in soils, protecting plant roots against root disease and promoting healthy soil structure.

A fertilization regimen should begin in the spring and repeat in the fall, when growth rates are elevated. It is not usually desirable to fertilize during the summer or winter months because this can "push growth" during times of heat and drought and will be ineffective during dormancy when roots cannot take up the nutrients. If a fertilizer application is desired, a liquid or granular organic fertilizer, can be applied at the manufacturer's recommended rates (rates vary by type of fertilizer and size of the plant). Most fertilizers contain a formulation of nitrogen, phosphorus, and potassium, but micronutrient deficiencies, which are often overlooked, can also cause plants to decline. It is a good idea to repeat soil testing regularly to identify missing nutrients in the soil and avoid over-fertilization; nutrients are sometimes present in the soil but unavailable to plants because of pH problems or other issues. These required nutrients can be obtained or made available through applications of compost, compost tea, or soil biostimulants rather than fertilizer, which can pollute the environment and should always be used with caution.

Once plants are established, after two to three years, fertilization can and should be eliminated, and organic matter should continue to be incorporated into the soil, either by the application of compost or by the decomposition of leaf litter. There has also been some more recent anecdotal evidence that supports applications of compost tea, made by steeping compost in water.

## THE AGING LANDSCAPE

Plants are not nonliving, static objects in the landscape, and they usually have very different forms and sizes when they are young than when they have reached maturity. As designers, we need to consider how the landscape will change as plants grow and mature: that a small sapling will take on a much different form than a mature shade tree, and that the unpredictability of environmental conditions will also play a role in shaping that tree. If these changes are not anticipated, and if plants are not maintained properly, the original design intent can be lost.

Like all living organisms, plants do not endure forever. The plant bed that was once shaded and sheltered by a mature tree can suddenly be exposed to higher light, wind, and water levels when that tree dies. New opportunities for fresh bursts of plant growth and changes in planting schemes are benefits of working with plants in the landscape. In flower gardens, especially, there are frequent opportunities for new introductions of perennials and annuals to promote color, interest, and change through the seasons. In these

7.17 The gardener at Kenarden in Bar Harbor, Maine, meticulously maintains this flower garden so it blooms consistently throughout the season while maintaining the designer's original intent for balance and structure.

instances, where plant beds are continually transforming, it is often beneficial for the designer to cultivate a good working relationship with the gardener, who often is much more knowledgeable about the site's specific microclimates and ways in which new plant introductions can work within the overall structure of the garden (Fig. 7.17).

Young landscapes only a season or two old have a different set of maintenance needs than mature landscapes, requiring special attention to water, nutrients, and soils to ensure the successful establishment of plants. Later, tree stakes and wires will need to be removed to allow plants to adapt to wind patterns and to avoid girdling as branch and trunk diameters increase and wires strangle and cut the supply of essential water and nutrients. Maintenance of mature landscapes

may require rejuvenation pruning, dividing of herbaceous perennials, monitoring of soil compaction, and adjustment of water and nutrient applications in order to keep older plants thriving and soils healthy.

With our improved understanding of botany, we can make better decisions about plant selection, examination, installation, and maintenance, and we can predict how plants will grow and interact with their environment. This knowledge can also assist us in manipulating the environment in order to promote specific patterns of growth. The following chapter further expands on this notion, describing ways in which plants can be physically manipulated to obtain particular growth habits that may further enhance our designs.

# 8

## MANIPULATING PLANT FORMS: PRUNING AND BEYOND

While the first task in planting design is to select the appropriate plants for any given design, plants can also be modified to meet specific needs. This chapter will describe the range of physical modifications available, from basic pruning for plant health and form to more extensive and ancient practices such as coppicing, topiary, and espalier for both form and function.

## BASIC PHYSICAL MODIFICATION OF PLANTS: PRUNING

Pruning is the selective removal of specific portions of a plant, and, in practical terms, we are most often referring to woody plants—trees, shrubs, and vines. Pruning is both a science and an art, and if done correctly and well it can enhance the beauty of a plant, highlight a design feature, and promote plant health and integrity. If done incorrectly, pruning can reduce the value of the plant at best, and leave a plant vulnerable to insects, disease, and premature death at worst.

Pruning should be a regular part of any maintenance schedule and should always be executed by a knowledgeable professional and with a specific purpose in mind. To this end, it is important for designers to have a basic understanding of proper pruning techniques and their purposes, enabling us to include pruning instruction in maintenance plans, select qualified professionals, and oversee pruning projects as necessary.

### BENEFITS

Pruning is important in maintaining plant health, reducing liability in the landscape, improving the vigor of older plantings, and enhancing design intent and plant appearance. Of the several approaches to pruning, each has its own outcome; a comprehensive maintenance plan that addresses the designer's vision for the landscape over time as well as any safety concerns related to the plantings will guide future caretakers of the landscape or garden in determining which pruning methods should be employed.

## Maintaining plant health

Pruning to maintain plant health should be an ongoing effort, evaluated annually at minimum and executed as needed.

- The removal of any dead, diseased, or damaged parts of a plant should be done as necessary, at any time of the year. Assessing a plant for these issues should be ongoing, and at minimum an annual task each spring, with periodic assessment throughout the season.
- Thinning a plant, or removing selected interior branches, can promote better light and air penetration, reduce the occurrence of fungal disease, and promote efficient photosynthesis. Thinning can also reduce the amount of shading for plants growing underneath; thinning trees and larger shrubs to allow some filtered sunlight to reach ground level helps stimulate the growth of understory plantings, thereby promoting a healthy landscape.
- The removal of suckers and water sprouts—vigorous upright shoots that occur at the base of the trunk or on branches, respectively—also promotes a healthier and more attractive plant, as these growths take up large amounts of nutrients and water that could otherwise be available to other parts of the plant.
- Generally, crossing branches should be removed as they may cause protective bark to rub off, providing an opportunity for insects or microorganisms to enter the plant.
- Sometimes pruning to balance roots and shoots is done at the time of transplanting, in order to promote healthy establishment of the plant, although there are two schools of thought on this practice. Those who advocate for root-to-shoot balance argue that the volume of roots lost during transplant can create an imbalance with the plant's shoots; the remaining roots cannot take up enough water and nutrients to support growth, causing the plant to decline. The opposing argument is that any pruning of healthy, living tissue can cause stunting and additional stress and that the plant will adjust its own growth without any intervention. Disproportionate shoot–to-root ratios can also occur if high amounts of nitrogen fertilizer are delivered to the plant; in this case, some pruning should be performed to help reestablish the balance and fertilizer regimens should be adjusted.

## Reducing liability in the landscape

Beyond these basic pruning requirements, another equally important reason to prune a plant is to reduce its potential liability in the landscape. Plants should always be pruned in a manner that promotes mechanical strength. This means identifying the main leader and scaffold limbs of a tree or large shrub and ensuring their proper angles of attachment and arrangement. This type of training should begin while the plant is young, ideally in the nursery and either prior to or at the time of plant selection. Limbs that are weakly attached or are damaged or diseased should always be removed to prevent them from falling and damaging structures or injuring pedestrians. Likewise, trees should be appropriately pruned in order to reduce utility line interference. Utility companies often haphazardly remove all or a portion of the main leader and scaffold branches of trees, a process called topping, in order to expose utility lines and reduce interference; this weakens the tree and increases its potential to fail and take down lines. A better practice is either to select tree species that will grow below utility line heights or to properly prune the tree, beginning when it is young, to avoid contact with the line. Effective pruning can also promote good vehicular and pedestrian visibility and movement; plants should never impede visibility on roadways or sidewalks and should be kept outside lines of sight and above head level of pedestrians.

## Improving the vigor of older plantings

As plants age, their growth and production of flowers and fruit begin to slow. In these instances, more intense pruning, if done properly, can improve the vigor of older plantings by promoting a burst of new growth. This type of pruning, called rejuvenation pruning, generally requires removing a higher percentage (sometimes as much as 80–90%) of shoots than normal in order to encourage a flush of new growth and can be very beneficial to the plant. The tolerance of plants to this type of intense pruning is genus and species specific, best suited to plants such as lilac, forsythia, and hibiscus. Similarly, removing selected branches, leaves, and buds that would otherwise take up nutrients and water can encourage a burst of growth in younger plants as well, especially newly transplanted plants that are trying to establish themselves in the landscape. Deadheading can also promote a flush of new growth, and in some instances a flush of new flowers as energy that would ordinarily go to producing fruit is redirected back to the plant.

## Enhancing design intent and plant appearance

Finally, we can prune a plant to increase its aesthetic value and support the design intent. As a general rule, enhancing the natural form of a plant from the time it is young is beneficial to both plant health and landscape aesthetic. This assumes a plant was selected for its natural form (extreme plant form manipulation is covered in the next section). Pruning can accentuate a particularly interesting branch that offers movement in the landscape, expose interesting bark, or draw attention to an attractive form, be it bold and upright or weeping and graceful. Keeping a set of sharp, clean pruners with you when you visit a site during or after planting installation allows you to lightly prune any plantings that may require it, in order to maintain the integrity of your design. Pruning can also help control the size and massing of plants, maintain plantings in scale with their surroundings, provide access to flowers and fruits by keeping these features within reach or at eye level, and open and direct views. Where plantings are meant to create enclosures, it is important for a designer's maintenance plan to identify where massing is meant to occur so that plants are allowed to grow together and form hedges or groupings, and not be pruned inadvertently into individual, separate objects. It is the designer's responsibility to communicate these intentions to those who will be maintaining the landscape.

## WHEN TO PRUNE

The timing of pruning can be just as important as technique. Dead, damaged, or diseased plant tissue should be removed as soon as it is identified, at any time of the year; if allowed to remain, it can provide an entry point for insects and disease. All other types of pruning listed above, as a general rule, should be performed in the spring, when plant growth is at its most active and plants have had enough time to heal before dormancy. Plants produce callus tissue over a wound and have a unique ability to wall off damaged tissue internally as well; these processes occur most rapidly in the spring. Late-season pruning should be avoided because the flush of new growth that will occur in reaction to the pruning will be vulnerable to winter injury.

There are many exceptions to the spring pruning rule. Some plant species can be damaged if pruned at this time; *Quercus* sp., for example, should not be pruned between April and July, when sap beetles are more likely to be attracted and spread oak wilt disease. Similarly, many deciduous trees should not be pruned while leafing out in spring, as plant reserves tend to be low and bark may slip easily and tear. Many other plants cannot tolerate cold snaps after an early spring planting and may be damaged if this occurs.

Other reasons for avoiding spring pruning may be largely aesthetic. For example, *Acer* and *Vitis* will bleed sap heavily if pruned in the early spring, although while unattractive, this bleeding will not harm the plant. Plants that produce flower buds on the previous season's wood, such as many species of hydrangea, should not be comprehensively pruned in spring (prior to flowering) or flower buds may be removed. In fact, questions about the blooming (or lack thereof) of hydrangeas are among the most common from clients. Because hydrangeas leaf out late in spring, maintenance crews and homeowners often prune the unsightly twigs at that time, and then wonder why they never produce a bloom. Likewise, early flowering species such as *Syringa*, *Forsythia*, and *Rhododendron* should be allowed to bloom before pruning, but should be pruned shortly after flowering, before new buds are set.

Thus it is important to keep in mind plants' bloom times when deciding when to prune; generally, we prune either immediately after flowering or in late winter, avoiding the removal of flower buds in order to prevent a reduction in blooms. In some cases, however, reducing in the number of flower buds can cause remaining flowers and fruits to grow larger, especially in mature plants, or can cause a burst of vegetative growth that may be beneficial to improved root-to-shoot ratios. Because of the wide variability in plants' tolerances and responses to the timing of pruning, we as designers should develop the habit of researching individual species before pruning is executed.

## WHERE TO PRUNE

When pruning deciduous trees, we must first identify the leader and main scaffold limbs, which are the primary limbs that form the structure of the canopy (Fig. 8.1). These major limbs provide the structural stability and aesthetic form of the plant. The scaffold limbs should be attached to the trunk at wide angles and be evenly spaced, radially, around the trunk. Any competing or improperly situated scaffold limbs should be removed. Secondly, any laterals (branches off the main scaffold limbs) that have grown taller than the leader should be pruned back to a junction with another branch, or to an outward facing bud. Finally, any suckers at the base of the trunk and water sprouts on the branches, as well as any diseased, broken, or crossing branches, should be removed.

When pruning shrubs, again first remove any dead, damaged, diseased, or crossing branches (Fig. 8.2). Next, identify any branches that are growing inward and shad-

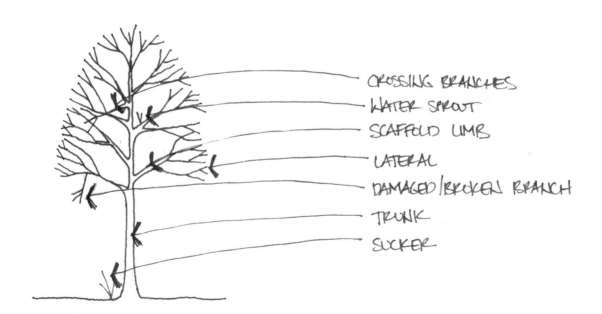

CROSSING BRANCHES
WATER SPROUT
SCAFFOLD LIMB
LATERAL
DAMAGED/BROKEN BRANCH
TRUNK
SUCKER

8.1 For pruning purposes, you should be familiar with these structures on a deciduous tree.

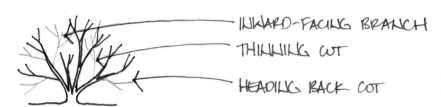

INWARD-FACING BRANCH

THINNING CUT

HEADING BACK CUT

8.2 The major types of pruning cuts on a shrub.

ing out the center of the shrub, as well as any branches that extend beyond the desired form of the shrub. Remember that tip pruning of branches will create a flush of growth beyond the cut due to apical dominance (see page 31), so identifying outward facing buds and cutting just beyond those buds will establish both good form and healthy density, letting sunlight and air penetrate the interior. If a plant has an opposite arrangement (see page 64), and buds are opposite one another on the stem, cuts should still be made above the buds, but the inward-facing bud may be removed. Cuts should always be made approximately ¼" above a bud and at a 45-degree angle.

Evergreen shrubs and trees generally do not require much pruning. They tend to have strong forms and grow more slowly than deciduous plants. They should, however, be periodically assessed for damaged or diseased branches as well as branches that are crossing or extending beyond the plant's desired form. When pruning is necessary in order to maintain form or plant health, broadleaved evergreen branches can be pruned at the junction with another branch, or back to a main leader. Needled evergreen shrubs, on the other hand, can be pruned either along the candle or along the branch, as described in the next section. Limbs of evergreen trees are

typically removed back to the main leader, a process called "limbing up" when applied to the lower branches, as it heightens the canopy so sunlight can penetrate below or so visibility is not impaired.

## HOW TO PRUNE

Because pruning creates open wounds on a plant, it is important to use clean, sharp tools. Tools should be cleaned periodically with a weak bleach solution, especially after cutting away diseased portions of a plant, to prevent the spread of harmful microorganisms. Do not paint pruning cuts with wound paints or other substances; while this was once a standard practice, recent studies have shown that paints can hinder the healing of wounds because they can trap microorganisms beneath the paint and they do not effectively seal out water and air, which can cause fungal growth and disease.

The correct location of a pruning cut on a deciduous tree branch is crucial to proper healing. It is imperative that the cut always be made just beyond the branch bark ridge, which is the swollen area of newer xylem tissue that is produced each year at the branch base (Fig. 8.3). This is a protective zone produced by the tree that, when left intact, prevents decay when a limb is removed either

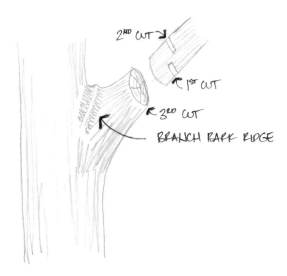

2ᴺᴰ CUT

1ˢᵀ CUT

3ᴿᴰ CUT

BRANCH BARK RIDGE

8.3 Proper pruning of a tree branch.

naturally or by pruning. Once the branch bark ridge is identified, the best practice is to use a three-cut method to remove branches that are over 1" in diameter: a first cut is made 1–2' out from the trunk on the underside of the branch, cutting only halfway through the branch; the second cut is made on the top side of the branch, all the way through (the branch should break naturally) and 1" beyond the first cut, to remove the weight of the branch and prevent tearing of the bark during the final cut; the third and final cut is made just beyond the branch bark ridge and is a smooth, angled cut that follows the line of the swollen ridge. Smooth, clean cuts promote healing.

When thinning, tip pruning, or heading back (cutting to a shorter length) a branch of a tree or shrub, always cut ¼" above either a node that contains an outward-facing bud, a junction with another branch, or the point of origin with the trunk, and at a 45-degree angle. As a general rule, these practices should be done together, where appropriate, as tip pruning and heading back can cause a flush of growth that requires some thinning in order to maintain appropriate shoot density. These practices can be helpful when shaping plants, but as with all pruning, some species are more tolerant than others. Many broadleaf evergreens, such as rhododendrons, do not generally respond well to heading back. Heading back should also not be confused with topping, the cutting back of the main leader of a tree; topping weakens trees and should not be practiced. Also, many plants are not tolerant of shearing, which haphazardly cuts each branch to the same length regardless of its location; shearing can encourage water sprouts to grow and create a "cloud" of dense canopy that will shade out the center of the plant, cause structural instability, and reduce sunlight and air penetration (Fig. 8.4). Certain plants, such as *Taxus* and *Buxus*, are tolerant of some shearing, although care should be taken to ensure the centers of these shrubs remain healthy and vigorous.

The proper way to prune needled evergreens, when required, is to pinch back the candles (new elongated growth that occurs at the tips of the branches) by 50% in the spring (Fig. 8.5). If necessary, larger branches can also be pruned back to a needled lateral shoot. Pruning back to a lateral within the inactive zone, where needles are no longer present, will prevent the branch from forming new tissue. Random branched evergreen species such as *Thuja, Juniperus,* and *Taxus* can be pruned back anywhere along their stems, as they contain latent buds that will sprout new growth no matter where they are cut.

8.4 Shearing certain types of shrubs can be detrimental to the plant, creating a cloud of foliage that light cannot penetrate.

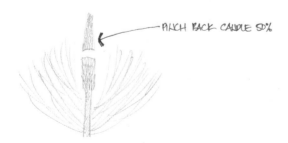

8.5 Proper pruning of an evergreen candle.

# EXTREME FORMS OF PHYSICAL MODIFICATION

While plants are most frequently pruned in order to enhance their natural form, there are some instances when more extreme forms of pruning are desired. The forms that are obtained from more intense pruning are often appropriate for formal designs, or are sometimes interjected into a contrasting, informal setting as a specimen or "folly." These types of pruning techniques require not only more intense levels of maintenance (sometimes requiring weekly pruning, depending on the plant's rate of growth and the client's expectations) but also a more comprehensive understanding of the plant species. Not every species can tolerate such intense pruning, and many species will not respond as desired, so it is important to know a plant's growth habits and tolerances.

## COPPICING AND POLLARDING

Coppicing and pollarding are among the most ancient horticultural practices, dating back to Neolithic times in England and France (4000–2500 BC; Fig. 8.6). Because both methods promote vigorous new growth, coppicing and pollarding were originally intended to produce firewood, basketwork, and poles. Today, however, these practices are used primarily for ornamental effect, as the stems produce an interesting geometric pattern in winter, especially when contrasted against the snow, the sky, or a blank wall. A very limited number of species can tolerate

8.6 Pollarding creates interesting patterns in the landscape. (Photo by Laura Knosp.)

to allow grazing animals to access pasture below. First, a young tree is selected with a well-branched canopy on a clear, unbranched trunk. Once the tree is established (approximately 6' tall) but before it reaches 4–5" in caliper, in late winter or early spring, the main stem is sawn through just above the lowest cluster of branches. Each of the remaining branches is then cut back to 1–3". New growth will result that is straight and vigorous. In order to maintain this form, the tree must be pruned every one to three years in late winter or early spring in order to shorten all the stems to within ½" to ¾" of the main stem. As the stems become overcrowded, some of the stems originating from the trunk can be removed. A variation on this type of pruning can also be performed on the ends of the main scaffold branches of a tree; once cut, the stem will form a knob of callus tissue that produces new, vigorous growth.

## PLEACHING

Pleaching, another horticultural practice with a long history, dates back to Tudor England (1485–1603 AD; Fig. 8.7). Often flanking the entry drives to grand estates, allées of pleached trees have always been a sign of status, since pleaching is an extremely labor-intensive practice. Pleaching creates a high hedge from the canopies of specific species of trees such as *Tilia*, *Carpinus*, *Fagus*, and *Ilex*. These hedges, which are made up of the intricately woven and carefully clipped branches of trees, sit high atop a row of straight, clear stems and can be prominent eye-catchers in

pollarding and coppicing, but these include some species of *Salix* and *Cornus*, both of which have colorful bark that adds to the ornamental effect. Pollarding is also used to grow trees in less space because it creates a more compact canopy.

Both coppicing and pollarding require hard pruning in the same location on the plant, and on a regular basis, resulting in a knob of swollen callus tissue that sprouts vigorous new growth. Coppicing involves cutting a tree or shrub back to the ground, usually annually, in order to obtain these vigorous young stems. Pollarding is similar, but is performed at the top of a tree's trunk, raising its shoots, and was originally intended the landscape, creating a solid mass of dense foliage that forces the eye to follow. Pleached trees can also create a high buffer to upper-story windows, while the regularly spaced trunks provide rhythm and a more open view at the ground level.

First, a support system is created from strong posts that are sunk 2–3' into the ground and are as tall as the intended mature hedge. Horizontal wooden strips or wires are then stretched between these posts in order to serve as supports to which branches will be tied. Three- to four-year-old trees are selected, with strong leaders and branches that begin at or near the height of the lowest horizontal members of the support structure and in a fairly flat plane. Once the trees are planted, these branches are tied to the horizontal supports and all shoots that appear on the trunks or grow away from the framework are removed. All other shoots are woven into the framework and tied. Once established, the pleached row of trees can be clipped as an ordinary hedge. Variations on this horticultural practice include arches or tunnels where two rows of trees on either side of a roadway or walkway are woven and tied at their tops.

8.7 Pleaching results in a high hedge on straight trunks. (Photo by Adam W. Turner.)

## TOPIARY

First practiced during Roman times, the art of topiary has traditionally been used to create architectural forms and geometric shapes from shrubs and trees in formal settings, often echoing formal architectural styles (Fig. 8.8). In more recent years, it has been popular to create animal forms and other more whimsical shapes that act as focal points or accents in landscapes that are not necessarily formal in style. Because of the intricacy of many topiary forms, as well as the intense clipping that is required, plant species with dense habits, pliable shoots, pruning tolerance, and small, evergreen leaves are best suited to this practice, including yew, laurel, and boxwood. Because topiaries are frequently used in containers, designers should choose cold-tolerant species or cultivars unless containers are to be brought indoors for the winter.

Creating topiary may involve clipping

leaves, needles, stems, or main branches, and can be done with or without a support system, depending on whether the plant itself provides the "scaffolding" structure. When an external support system is used, it can be formed into a shape that roughly approximates the form of the finished product. Plant stems are tied to the training form until they maintain their position. Once the form is established, frequent clipping and/or shearing is required for the life of the plant, sometimes as often as every few weeks, depending on the plant's rate of growth. A faster and easier approach to topiary is to train fast-growing ivy to a wire frame in the desired shape; this technique requires little maintenance beyond tying new shoots to the frame.

## ESPALIER

Popular during the Middle Ages, espalier is the training of trees and shrubs so the branches lie on one plane (Fig. 8.9). Historically, this horticultural practice was used with fruit trees in order to keep them small, to fit within smaller yards and gardens. Because these espaliered plants were generally supported against a wall, the reflective heat kept fruit production high. Today, espalier is more often an ornamental practice. Espaliered trees and shrubs can be trained against large expanses of windowless walls to provide architectural interest, or along fences or trellises to create interesting boundaries to garden spaces. Fruit trees remain the best selection for this practice, although other spur-bearing species, such as *Pyracantha*, *Crataegus*, and *Chaenomeles*, can also be used.

A support structure made up of posts and horizontal members is constructed to support the growth of the espalier, and appropriate plants are selected and trained to it. Each winter, the main leader is cut back to just above the level where the next horizontal tier of branches is desired; this process of cutting back the leader directs energy into the lateral branches. The two strongest lateral branches are tied onto the horizontal member of the structure and the leader is allowed to grow to the next horizontal tier. The following win-

8.8 Topiary brings whimsical, geometric shapes into the landscape.

8.9 Espalier adds interest to a blank wall.

## LAYERING

Some species of plants can form adventitious roots from their stems if the stems come into contact with the soil. The new plants that form are still attached to the parent plant, but they eventually detach and survive on their own and can be left in place or transplanted to another location. This form of vegetative propagation can be an economical and informal way to create dense colonies of plants for buffering, screening, or otherwise identifying the boundary of a space. For some species of plants, this process occurs naturally, while other species require some mechanical wounding to the stem and/or physical immersion into the soil.

There are several types of layering practices that work for different species of plants. Simple layering requires sharply bending a flexible stem to the ground in early spring and covering it partially with soil. The terminal 6–12" of the stem is left exposed and orientated vertically outside the soil level. Plants that are good candidates for this type of layering include climbing roses, forsythia, rhododendron, azalea, and honeysuckle. Tip layering is similar to simple layering, but requires inserting the tip of a shoot into the soil and covering it completely. Once the offshoot plant roots it will grow upward and become a new plant. Plants that are good candidates for this type of layering include raspberries and blackberries. Serpentine layering is also similar to simple layering, but several layers can be achieved from a single stem (Fig. 8.10). A long, flexible branch can

ter it is once again cut, and the two strongest lateral branches are again tied into the next horizontal support member. This process repeats until the desired form is complete. To maintain the espalier, the main leader is kept clear and all shoots that grow from the horizontal branches are pruned to three leaves above the basal cluster in order to keep the pattern recognizable. A traditional espalier is symmetrical, with pairs of branches of equal length occurring nearly opposite one another, but the many variations on this form include fan-shape, cordon (menorah shape), and basket weave.

8.10 Serpentine layering can create a row or massing of plantings from one parent plant.

be bent and inserted, with alternate sections covered by soil and left exposed. Each section, whether covered or exposed, should contain at least one bud. Good candidates for this type of layering include *Wisteria*, *Clematis*, and *Vitis*.

## GRAFTING

Grafting is another form of vegetative propagation that has been used for thousands of years and can be very useful in design (Fig. 8.11). The root system (rootstock) of one plant is fused with the shoot system (scion) of another in order to obtain the beneficial properties of both. Typically, the rootstock is selected for its dwarfing properties or cold tolerance. For example, most apple trees are grafted onto dwarfing rootstocks in order to make harvesting easier and allow for more trees to be planted in closer proximity one to another. Rootstocks can also be selected in order to provide a strong, tall trunk for particular ornamental shrubs or trees such as *Salix* and *Rosa*, turning what is normally a multistemmed or weakly stemmed plant into a standard on a high, straight stem. The scion, or shoot system of the graft, is generally selected for its ornamental characteristics.

8.11 Grafting can create standards out of plants that are naturally a shrub form.

In order for successful grafting to take place, the vascular cambia (the thin layer of actively dividing cells responsible for producing vascular tissue—xylem and phloem—in the plant) of the rootstock and that of the scion must be placed in contact with each other so they will fuse and form a continuous tissue that can transport water and nutrients throughout the plant. When specifying grafted plants, designers should take extra care to inspect plants at the point of the graft, as this can be a weak point if the graft was not successful, leading to later problems with stability or susceptibility to insects and disease.

# 9

## CHOOSING WOOD FOR HARDSCAPE

Hardscape—the non-living, man-made aspects of our designs such as driveways, walkways, structures, and decks—also plays an important role in design decisions, helping to extend interior space outdoors and informing our plant selection.

Lumber, in particular, is a material that can dramatically influence the look of a design. For example, when it comes to flooring for a deck, a designer might select a wood quite different from that used in cabinetry, moldings, furniture, an exterior trellis, or a building frame. If wood is going to be stained, exposing its grain, the choice might be quite different from a wood that is going to be painted, or hidden behind drywall. Application often dictates the choice of wood.

In this chapter we will explore the use of wood as a building material that complements landscape design treatments, and explain how to determine which type is best suited to achieving the function and look you want.

## KEY CHARACTERISTICS OF WOOD

How do we go about selecting the appropriate wood for a particular design feature? Understanding the botany behind three key characteristics of tree trunks is helpful in evaluating the many choices available to designers: heartwood or sapwood, springwood or summerwood, and softwood or hardwood.

### HEARTWOOD AND SAPWOOD

The bulk of a tree's trunk is comprised of wood, or xylem. As a tree ages, the trunk diameter expands horizontally as the plant creates more xylem and phloem cells to support its growth and increase the girth of its trunk. In very old trees, the innermost wood or xylem cells may contain decay-resistant chemical compounds, as well as waste products, which change their color and density. These portions of wood are called heartwood and are highly valued in furniture making and exposed surfaces of interior construction, as well as for exterior applications where rot and pest resistance are necessary. Younger wood that has not yet been impregnated with these hardening substances is often lighter in color and is called the sapwood.

## SPRINGWOOD AND SUMMERWOOD

If we were to cut a cross-section of a tree trunk, we would see that a large portion of the center consists of a lighter-colored wood, the xylem, and a darker, thinner outer ring, the phloem, and finally a rougher, exfoliating, or spongier outer covering, the cork or bark (Fig. 9.1). Within the circle of xylem, we would also see what are called annual rings, each representing one year of growth. These rings form because of the very regu-

lar growth rate of a woody plant during the seasons of a year. In the spring, plants grow much more quickly because of the availability of water and nutrients, and hence the cells that are developed during this time are larger and more abundant. The wood (or xylem) created during this time of year is appropriately called the springwood. In summer, when more droughts occur and water and nutrients are less availabile, cellular growth slows and developing cells are smaller and less abundant. This wood is called summerwood. In a cross-section of a trunk, the springwood appears slightly lighter in color and the summerwood slightly darker. From these very regular ring patterns, one can determine not only the age of a tree but also which years were drier than others, or which years included climatic changes that caused variations in the patterns of the rings. In this way, annual rings act as a record of weather patterns in various regions of the world. These rings are also very important to designers because they form the beautiful and varying grains of wood that are so valued in furniture-grade timber.

## SOFTWOOD AND HARDWOOD

Whether a given wood is a softwood or a hardwood determines its strength, durability, and cost. Beyond these two categories, further selection can be made based on the unique, aesthetic characteristics of the wood. While the terms softwood and hardwood might lead one to believe that they have something to do with the physical strength of the wood, such is not always the case; these terms are botanical

9.1 Cross-section of a tree trunk.

distinctions. Softwood is used to describe the wood from conifers, or gymnosperms, which tend to grow in colder regions, such as pine, redwood, and spruce. This wood tends to be less durable but faster growing and forms the bulk of the wood used by humans. Because it tends to be paler in color, close grained, and "knotty," it is not as highly valued aesthetically and is primarily used in framing and building components, where it is not visible. When it is used in finish construction, it is generally painted. While not necessarily softer than hardwood (there are some hardwoods, such as balsa, that are softer than softwoods), the wood from these trees does tend to be soft.

Hardwood is used to describe the wood from angiosperms that generally grow in temperate or tropical climates, such as oak, teak, mahogany, and ash. These woods contain cells that have high levels of lignin, and they are more valuable as construction materials because they tend to be stronger, denser, and more resistant to decay. Hardwoods are also often used in finish carpentry because they are more aesthetically appealing. When a designer describes the "beauty" of a piece of furniture-grade wood, he or she is often describing the color and grain, which is a species-specific quality that can also be highly variable within the same species.

## ADDITIONAL CONSIDERATIONS

When a tree is felled, the trunk is run through a machine that cuts it into pieces usable for construction. When the cut is made parallel along the length of the log, it is called plain sawn. This particular type of cut reveals the full character of the wood, including the knots (which mark the beginning of a branch) and other variations in color and pattern of the grain. When a timber is cut radially, it is called quarter sawn. This results in wood of a more uniform texture and color. When a timber is cut across the grain, in cross-section, it is called end grain and is the hardest and most durable cut. Even within the same species, there can be great variation in grain, density, and durability from tree to tree. Therefore, timber is graded according to appearance, with the most select lumber having the fewest defects, and primarily being cut from the heartwood. All designers who work with timber products should have a basic understanding of the finer timber characteristics, including grain pattern, color, density, machinability (ease with which it can be cut and finished), potential finishes, and durability (rot and insect resistance).

## EVALUATING COMMERCIAL WOODS

Some of the most commonly used commercial woods and their key characteristics are listed below:

*Ash*: Native to North America, this wood is grayish-brown, sometimes with a red tinge, and is generally paler in color than other woods. It has a straight grain and coarse texture, with excellent density, strength,

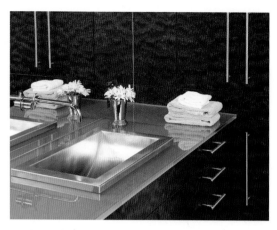

9.2 Figured babinga veneer paneling. (Photo by Marcus Gleysteen.)

and durability. It stains well, has very good machinability, and is used to make furniture, baseball bats, cabinets, paneling, veneer, and flooring.

*Babinga*: Native to Africa, this wood is medium red-brown with lighter reddish-purple veins. It has tight, fine veination that varies from straight to heavily figured, depending on the cut. A moderately durable wood, babinga has good machinability and is easily stained. It is primarily used in veneer, cabinetry, furniture, and paneling (Fig. 9.2).

*Bamboo*: Not a true wood but rather a grass with woody characteristics, bamboo is among the fastest-growing plants in the world and is ready to harvest in five years. Boards are made from layers of bamboo strips, laminated under high pressure, which makes for interesting patterns and variable colors. Being both extremely strong and durable, it is used in flooring and wall cladding.

*Beech*: Native to North America, this wood is reddish-brown, with a slightly coarse, straight grain and a fine, even texture. A dense, heavy wood, beech machines well at slow speeds. It is easy to work with, stains well, and is durable, and it is used in furniture, cabinetry, and flooring.

*Birch*: Native to North America, this wood has light yellow sapwood and reddish-brown heartwood with a straight, close grain and a fine, even texture. It can chip if machining is not sharp, but will take finish very well. Not a strong or particularly dense or durable wood, it is typically used to face plywood or as a veneer.

*Cedar*: Native to North America, this wood is reddish in color and has a delicate fragrance and a fine, even grain. Lightweight but durable, its cellular structure is such that it has great thermal and soundproofing characteristics and is easy to machine. Because it is aromatic, it also is pest resistant and therefore used for drawer linings, linen closets, chests, furniture, shingles, and exterior trimwork, fencing and outdoor structures.

*Cherry*: Native to North America, this wood is red to reddish-brown in color with a fine, straight grain and smooth texture. Easy to work with and moderately dense, this wood is easy to carve and finish, and is used in flooring, furniture, cabinetry, veneer, paneling, and boat interiors. Furniture makers rarely stain this wood because of its natural beauty (Fig. 9.3).

*Chestnut*: American chestnut, native to North America, is a very strong, durable, and easily worked wood that has been all but wiped out by blight, making it scarce and expensive. Blond to brown in color, with

9.3 Natural cherry cabinets and quarter sawn oak floor.
(Photo by Marcus Gleysteen.)

a closed, straight grain, it can also have tiny holes caused by pinworm, resulting in the highly valued "wormy" chestnut. It is used in furniture, cabinets, flooring, paneling, and veneer.

*Cyprus*: Native to Australia, this wood is golden, cream, or brown in color with tight grain and prevalent knots. Like cedar, it has a delicate fragrance due to natural oils that make it somewhat resistant to attack by insects. It is highly durable, takes finish well, and is easy to work with. It is used in flooring, exposed finishes, and cabinetry.

*Douglas Fir*: Native to North America, this extremely strong, durable wood is typically used as structural lumber in framing.

It is easy to work and finish and has a close, straight grain with a reddish-amber color, making it valued in exposed beam construction as well as furniture, cabinetry, flooring, and trimwork.

*Ebony*: Native to Africa and considered an endangered species, this very dense, durable, hardwood is thought to be the blackest wood that grows. It has a straight, very finely textured grain and is difficult to work. It is used in piano keys, musical instrument pieces, and inlay.

*Elm*: Native to North America, this very strong wood has been nearly wiped out by Dutch elm disease. Moderately dense, it has an open, close grain varying from straight to wavy, and a color that varies from cream to greenish- or purplish-brown. It machines and finishes fairly well and is used in furniture and cabinets, although it is scarce.

*Hickory*: Native to North America, this wood is brown to reddish-brown in color, with a straight or wavy grain and a somewhat coarse texture. It is strong, durable, and difficult to work, with although it stains well. It is used in cabinetry, flooring, veneer, and sports equipment such as rackets and clubs.

*Ipe*: Native to South and Central America, this wood is similar in appearance to teak, especially in the way it weathers, but without the oily finish and high price. It is extremely resistant to pests and decay, making it useful in outdoor applications, especially decking. Being both durable and hard, it is extremely difficult to machine.

*Mahogany*: Native to Africa and considered endangered, this dark, reddish-brown

9.4 Mahogany exterior door. (Photo by Marcus Gleysteen.)

hardwood is medium grained, pest resistant, strong, and easy to carve and finish. It is used in furniture, flooring, cabinets, decking, and outdoor structures (Fig. 9.4).

*Maple*: Native to North America, this moderately dense wood is creamy white with a reddish tinge and a straight or wavy grain. Difficult to work with and stain, this durable wood is used in flooring, furniture, paneling, and veneer (Fig. 9.5).

*Oak*: Native to North America, this hard, dense, durable wood is coarse grained, brown to gray with a reddish tinge. It stains and machines well and is used in flooring, furniture, cabinetry, trim, and veneer. It is not recommended for exterior use.

*Pine*: Native to North America, this softwood is pale and honey-colored, inexpensive, and soft. It is typically used in framing and is harvested (sapwood) while it is still young. Heart pine, on the other hand, is reclaimed heartwood from old-growth trees. This wood was used in homes and factories in the late nineteenth and early twentieth centuries. and the boom in construction caused the old-growth forests of North America to be all but

9.5 Broadleaf maple slab with de-barked "live edge." (Photo by Marcus Gleysteen.)

wiped out. Today, pine is being reclaimed and recycled from these old buildings and used in new construction, as it has rich rose, copper, and burgundy tones and is strong and durable.

*Poplar*: Native to North America, this wood is creamy white to greenish-yellow in color, with a straight grain and fine texture. Because of its greenish color, it is usually painted. Tough and easy to machine and finish, it is generally used in trim, furniture framing, drawers, crates, and plywood (Fig. 9.6).

*Spanish Cedar*: Neither Spanish nor a cedar, this wood is native to Central and South America and because of its high cost is almost exclusively used in high-end homes. It is pale pinkish-brown becoming dark reddish-brown, with a straight grain, moderately coarse texture, and high strength and durability. Easy to work but difficult to finish, it is used in furniture, cabinets, paneling, flooring, boats, veneer, and exterior trim.

*Sycamore*: Native to North America,

this wood is dark brown to reddish-brown in color, with an irregular grain and uniform texture. It is easily machined and finished but not usually highly valued aesthetically, so it is inexpensive. It is primarily used in furniture framing, drawers, and crates, though it can sometimes be used in cabinetry and paneling.

*Teak*: Native to Costa Rica, this tropical hardwood is considered endangered. It has a uniform, golden brown color without markings, and a straight to slightly wavy grain. Oily to the touch, this wood stains and machines moderately well and is very durable. Because of its weather resistance, it is often used in exterior applications such as outdoor furniture, decking, and boats, but is also used in

9.6 Painted poplar trim with figured mahogany drawer. (Photo by Marcus Gleysteen.)

interior furniture, cabinetry, and flooring.

*Walnut*: Native to North America, this wood has a rich dark brown to purplish-black color and straight to slightly wavy grain. A lightweight wood, walnut is very easily worked and has unsurpassed finishing capabilities. Because of its strength and durability, it is often used in furniture, cabinetry, countertops, and flooring, as well as veneer.

*Wenge*: Native to Africa, this hardwood is dark brown in color with a close, fine, almost black grain. With moderate machining and finishing, this wood is very durable and therefore used in flooring, cabinetry, and decorative paneling.

For centuries, humans have used wood in the construction of structures for shelter, worship, commerce, and travel. Because wood is a living, versatile, and "renewable" resource, it has become the staple of the construction industry, often making up 80–90% of the structure of a building minus the foundation. Wood is not only the most common building material, but also the most economical and it leaves the smallest carbon footprint (it is the "greenest" building material by a factor of 2). It also evokes an emotional response in people, often being described as "warm," "comforting," and having great "character." But as "green" and abundant as wood remains in comparison to other, inorganic construction materials, forest populations are declining. We collectively consume timber at a rate ten times faster than it can be replaced, especially hardwoods, which grow more slowly than softwoods and thus are slower to be replenished. Today, over 80% of the world's ancient forests have been destroyed. As a sustainable practice, more designers are specifying composite woods (plywood, medium density fiberboard, chipboard, and other processed woods formed from wood particles and glue) because they use a higher percentage of the tree (less waste) than solid wood, which only uses parts of the trunk. Composite woods are also less susceptible to changes in humidity and temperature and are cheaper in terms of materials cost. Designers are also increasingly specifying non-exotic or non-endangered species, as well as wood from managed plantations. Another practice of increasing popularity is the use of salvaged or reclaimed wood in building construction, as with heart pine. These timbers are salvaged from ships, museums, mill buildings, barns, banks, public buildings, etc., planed, and reused in new construction. They often exhibit unmatched character and unique characteristics.

These practices are only a few of the ways designers can help promote environmental responsibility and sustainability. The following chapter discusses additional ways we can promote "green" practices in design.

# 10

## NATURE'S SOLUTIONS: GREEN DESIGN STRATEGIES

The concept of sustainability is not a new one. Over the years, it has been discussed under many different names, such as sustainable design, green design, and ecological design, but its basic goals have remained the same: to minimize destruction of the environment by designing to meet current needs without compromising the ability of future generations to thrive. Sustainable design respects living processes, maintains species diversity, minimizes the depletion of resources and habitats, and preserves natural cycles.

While there are many topics that can be covered within the realm of "green design," this chapter addresses a handful of trends as they relate to botany, including the use of plants and open space within the built environment, sensitive materials selection, biomimicry, green roofs, vertical gardens, and harvesting rainwater for irrigation.

## ABOUT LEED CERTIFICATION

In an attempt to promote a sustainable built environment, the U.S. Green Building Council (USGBC) developed the LEED (Leadership in Energy and Environmental Design) program as a means of assessing and rating the sustainability of built works. The system allocates points to each sustainable practice used in the design and construction of a project, including those discussed in this chapter. Six different rating system programs have been developed for different project types, including new construction, schools, core and shell, commercial interior, existing building, and neighborhood development.

These rating systems take into consideration five key areas of human and environmental health—Sustainable Sites, Water Efficiency, Energy and Atmosphere, Materials and Resources, and Indoor Environmental Quality—and give a rating based on the effectiveness of each. Of these five impact areas, three are applicable to landscape design, making up to 40% of points obtainable through landscape-based decisions. Within the Sustainable Sites criteria, landscape design that reduces impact to open space, manages stormwater, utilizes regionally appropriate planting, and reduces erosion and heat island effect receives the most points. Water Efficiency is another key impact area, and selecting water efficient plantings or using alternative irrigation systems can help gain points. The third key impact area that can be influenced by landscape design is Materials and Resources. Points can be acquired by utilizing certified wood that has been harvested from environmentally friendly practices, rapidly renewable resources, or regional or recycled materials. As we will see in the sections that follow, nearly every one of these credit-gaining requirements can be achieved with plants.

Designers can certify their projects by submitting an application that documents compliance with the requirements of the LEED rating system and paying registration and certification fees (more information can be found at the USGBC website). While the rating system is voluntary, it can be quite valuable from the consumer's standpoint, in the peace of mind derived from knowing that building or development is environmentally sensitive, and from the developer's standpoint as well, in creating a more marketable end product.

While many designers have embraced the LEED system (it is the only "green" program with a national scope that has been accepted by private organizations and local/federal governments alike), it is not the only system designed to assess sustainability—there are many others at more local levels—and it has been subject to some controversy. Critics argue that the outcomes of the system haven't been studied or measured thoroughly enough, that some of its directives may actually result in more energy consumption, and that the points are not weighted appropriately (although this last complaint has recently been addressed in the creation of regional weighting of point values). Some designers argue that the methods they have been using for years do a better job than the standardized system LEED. While we may see additional fine-tuning of the program, it can be used today as a tool in helping to create more sustainable design.

## MITIGATING ENVIRONMENTAL PROBLEMS WITH PLANTS AND OPEN SPACE

More often than not, when we are called upon to create gardens and landscapes we must respond not only to aesthetic design challenges but also to problems presented by the site. We can use plants' functionality to mitigate common environmental problems, particularly those found in the built environment of urban areas. Plants have been shown to moderate temperature fluctuations; reduce stormwater runoff, pollution, erosion, and noise; provide animal habitat; and improve people's aesthetic and psychological experience of the built environment. Designers involved in any type of development, from a single-family residence to a multiacre community, should advocate for the establishment of green space in order to promote a more sustainable built environment and a healthier ecosystem.

## MODERATING TEMPERATURE FLUCTUATIONS

Because plants have the unique ability to moderate the microclimates around them, designers can utilize them to influence human environmental comfort and even reduce energy consumption and costs. Human comfort is very much dependent on temperature. Plants are able to affect temperature in two ways. First, as water transpires through their stomata and evaporates off the surface of their leaves, plants not only increase humidity but also reduce the air temperature around them. Water requires heat energy from its surroundings in order to convert from a liquid to a gas, and it takes that heat energy from the surrounding air, thereby cooling it. Because water does not fluctuate in temperature as readily as air, the more humid environment created by plant materials reduces variability in temperatures.

Second, plants' leaves reflect light, particularly green light, and absorb other wavelenghts for use in photosynthesis. As solar radiation is reflected, ambient temperature is reduced, which is why the temperature

10.1 Plants provide environmental comfort in the urban environment.

around materials such as asphalt, which absorbs solar radiation and releases it as heat energy, is much higher than the temperature around more reflective materials such as plants. Plants also reduce solar radiation by providing shade (Fig. 10.1). In temperate climates, planting deciduous trees provides shade (lower temperatures) in the summer months and solar radiation (heat) in the winter months when the trees lose their leaves. The form and foliage density of a plant affects its ability to provide shade. Plants with simple, broad leaves tend to cast more shade than those with smaller, compound leaves.

10.2 Plants can be used as windbreaks.

Because air movement, or wind, has a direct influence on extremes in temperature and humidity, it can also affect environmental comfort levels for humans and animals. The challenges of a windy site can often be met effectively with the use of well-chosen plant material. Designers can use plants as windbreaks, with the potential to reduce wind velocity by 75–80%, depending on the height, density, shape, and width of the windbreak (Fig. 10.2). As a general rule, windbreaks reduce wind at a distance two to three times their height, with the most effective wind reduction occurring closer to the windbreak; at distances approaching three times the height of the windbreak, some breeze may occur, which may be desired in south-facing, warmer microclimates. The effectiveness of a windbreak is also correlated to its density (the denser the break, the more effective), its shape (U- and L-shaped breaks prevent winds from whipping around the ends more effectively than straight breaks), and its width (the wider the break, the wider the area of protection). Windbreaks are also effective in alleviating snowdrifts, although the plantings selected should have high tolerances to heavy snow loads. Good choices are pyramidal-shaped conifers, which have both flexible branches and shapes that help shed snow.

## REDUCING STORMWATER RUNOFF, EROSION, POLLUTION, AND NOISE

Built environments have significant detrimental effects on drainage patterns. Acres of impervious surfaces created by roadways, parking lots, rooftops, and other hard surfaces force stormwater to shed very quickly, creating flood hazards and collecting particulate matter as the water travels back into waterways. Planting beds and vegetated retention ponds can both slow the rate at which stormwater travels across the surface by reducing surface smoothness and filter out the particulate pollutants before they enter groundwater or waterways.

Vegetative cover also reduces the impact of rainwater on the surface of soils by protecting and covering it, slowing soil erosion. As roots spread and grow through the soil, they hold soil particles in place and prevent them from washing away and polluting waterways. It is particularly important for designers working at new construction sites or areas with steep slopes to advocate for a comprehensive practice of planting and maintaining groundcover or other plant material in order to prevent erosion (Fig. 10.3).

Plants also have the unique ability to remove toxic gases and particulate pollutants from the atmosphere. Some solids, such as smoke and dust, can be adsorbed by leaves, while others stick to the blades, especially if

10.3 Plants help prevent erosion.

trichomes are present, and are washed away by rainfall. But if levels of pollutants become too high, they can become toxic to plant material, and thus plants can become indicators of lethal levels of pollutants in the atmosphere.

Plants can be used to buffer noise in much the same way that they can be used to redirect wind. Their effectiveness is dependent on the intensity and frequency of the noise, with higher frequency sound waves being most easily abated by plant materials and lower frequencies by soil. As with windbreaks, the height, width, and density of the planting will have an effect on its success in reducing noise, as will its proximity and location to the source point. Also, groundcover is much more effective at reducing noise pollution than are hard surfaces, which tend to reflect sound waves rather than absorb them.

## PROVIDING ANIMAL HABITAT

All buildings create change within previously existing ecosystems. Their construction displaces habitat and creates environments less conducive to native flora and fauna, resulting in a patchwork of regions within the larger ecosystem where certain species of wildlife cannot exist. These areas create breaks in natural migration patterns, preventing wildlife from moving freely through the landscape.

As designers, we can create open space within the built environment, corridors of green that help facilitate the movement of wildlife and improve the health of the ecosystem. Just as plants modify the microclimate and make conditions more comfortable for humans, they provide favorable habitat for animals as well. Designers can choose plants to provide animals with food, shelter, and protection from the elements and from potential predators.

We must be aware, however, that in certain situations, we will not want to attract certain species of wildlife (squirrels and other rodents, for example), particularly within urban environments. Through careful plant selection and proper maintenance practices, planting beds can be kept clear of the kinds of debris and overgrown ground covers that can be used as nesting sites by rodents. For example, planting beds can be periodically thinned to allow sunlight to penetrate and reduce hiding places for rodents, and branches can be pruned within 3–6' of building facades to prevent rodents from getting inside. Dense groundcovers, such as bamboo and honeysuckle, should be avoided in favor of thinner, lower-growing groundcovers such as creeping thyme, ajuga, and mondo grass. Lawn areas should also be kept trimmed. Food is a major attractant for rodents, so areas should be kept clear of dropped fruits, nuts, and seeds, as well as any human food garbage or pet food, which should be stored in tight, metal containers. Similarly, composts that utilize meats such as fish or chicken should be avoided in areas where rodents are particularly invasive.

Plants can also be used to help restore damaged ecosystems if they are chosen and placed carefully in order to mimic natural systems. To successfully provide the most beneficial green space for a particular site, designers should conduct a comprehensive site and ecological analysis that evaluates the natural patterns of the landscape. We should aim to unify built environment and landscape as much as possible, preserving existing patterns and processes. Any change, no matter how slight, can have far-reaching effects on the ecosystem as a whole. A site should not be defined merely by its legal boundaries, but by the contours of patterns within the greater ecosystem. In some instances, a designer may conclude from such site analysis that an alternative site should be selected.

## IMPROVING THE AESTHETIC AND PSYCHOLOGICAL EXPERIENCE

While designers have the capability to help heal the environment through thoughtful and responsible design practices, we also have the opportunity to heal the minds and soothe the souls of those who enjoy our gardens and landscapes.

The healing power of nature has been appreciated for centuries. Therapeutic gardens are thought to have first appeared in Europe during the Middle Ages, as people came to understand the benefits the outdoors had on human mental and physical well being. The eighteenth century marked a revival of both "therapeutic" gardens and "pastoralism," in which nature and gardens were thought of as places of bodily and spiritual restoration. The late nineteenth and early twentieth centuries, which brought industrialization and overcrowding in cities, marked the beginnings of the parks movement in the United States, advocated and advanced by Frederick Law Olmsted, the father of American landscape architecture. Olmsted strongly believed that the artificial patterns of the city were harmful to man's mental and nervous systems and caused social and psychological ills. He believed that the natural environment had curative qualities that could ameliorate these negative effects, and he argued that parks and green spaces should be incorporated within the fabric of cities, to act as "lungs" for the city and help heal man of his physical and psychological ailments (Fig. 10.4).

It can be argued today that these open

10.4 Green spaces act as "lungs" within our urban environments.

green spaces continue to be imperative in our urban and built environments, not only as venues for active recreation but also as places to relax and enjoy the benefits of nature in an otherwise chaotic concrete jungle. There is no doubt that natural areas have a positive influence on the human psyche, allowing the eye, as well as the mind, to wander and separate from the chaos, distractions, and obligations of our everyday lives. Growing research supports the concept that any amount of green space, from a small urban pocket park to a large multiacre arboretum, can have a positive influence on the human psyche. Similarly, any degree of interaction, from a vigorous hike through the forest to the view out an office window, can result in a positive outcome. Providing urban dwellers with access to nature offers them opportunities for enjoying clearer heads, better concentration, and faster recovery from illness.

## GREEN ROOFS AND VERTICAL GARDENS

One of the most rapidly developing fields in design today is the planting of green roofs. Roofs represent 40–50% of the impervious surface in urban areas and contribute greatly to the urban heat island effect and stormwater pressures. Historically in the United States, roofs have largely been an ignored surface, but a growing trend has designers embracing the opportunity to improve the aesthetic and environmental quality of our cities by paying more attention to this abundant real estate (Fig. 10.5). Research supports the trend, demonstrating that green roofs can result in significant reductions in stormwater runoff, improved runoff quality, longer roof life due to reduced heat and UV exposure, and a reduction in heating and cooling costs. While the initial construction costs may be as much as two to four times higher, these roofs can last up to seven times longer than their conventional counterparts, and the long-term savings in HVAC costs can be substantial. Direct and indirect costs can be measured in a number of ways, and it may be argued that green roofs make good financial as well as environmental sense.

When the concept of roof gardens first took hold in this country, the practice was generally restricted to container gardening or to

10.5 Green roofs provide an opportunity to bring greenery into otherwise underutilized space in cities.

spreading a layer of ordinary soil on a rooftop, requiring substantial roof strength to support the load. Since then, however, new technologies have enabled great advancements. Lightweight soils have been developed that can support root growth at 6" or shallower depths and within the load limits of many existing rooftops. Advancements in thermal insulation, waterproofing membranes, and filter mats now greatly reduce failures of these green roofs due to root penetration or compromised drainage systems (Fig. 10.6).

The design of green roofs has also changed and developed. Beyond the "intensive" ornamental roof gardens meant to be accessed by people, designers are now also creating "extensive" green roofs intended to contribute to the sustainability of the building and the urban environment, some meant only to be viewed from above and others not at all. These less elaborate, more functional green roofs require only a thin substrate layer and minimal maintenance and may consist of no more than a blanket of low plantings on a flat surface. Green roofs also create the opportunity for water recycling, water storage, and the harnessing of wind and solar energy for use in the buildings they service. A successful green roof requires careful plant selection, however, usually for drought and wind tolerance and ability to survive extreme fluctuations in temperatures (Fig. 10.7).

10.6 New advances in green roof design allow for greater variety in planting.

10.7 Green roofs require careful plant selection. (Photo by Laura Knosp.)

10.8 Vertical gardens can greatly improve the aesthetics and environmental quality of the built environment.

seen by a wide range of users, vertical gardens have much more visibility and can create aesthetic interest, especially where little architectural detail is present (Fig. 10.8).

The components of vertical gardens are very similar to those of roof gardens: they require a footing of soil in which roots can grow, waterproofing, and a lightweight substrate. Unlike roof gardens, which grow on a horizontal plane, vertical gardens require a framework that will hold soil in place and support plantings. Several modular systems are available commercially, offering convenience and ease of installation, and recent advancements in irrigation systems help reduce the limits on plant growth (Fig. 10.9). Just as with green roofs, proper plant selection is critical to the success of these gardens. Plants must be drought tolerant, as buildings often cast a shadow where rainfall is prevented from

Vertical gardens or planted walls, another recent trend in green design, can have similarly positive environmental effects on the urban landscape. Like rooftops, the facades of buildings represent a surface in the urban environment that has been underutilized in planting design and has great potential to improve both the aesthetic and environmental quality of the built environment. Like green roofs, planted walls can reduce fluctuations in temperature, thereby lowering heating and cooling costs; protect building surfaces from UV and weather damage, thereby reducing maintenance costs; and provide a noise barrier. While roof gardens may or may not be

10.9 Vertical gardens can also be used in interior spaces.

reaching the roots, and most integrated wall systems provide little soil medium in which to hold moisture. Maintenance is imperative to the success of vertical gardens, including regular applications of water, soil amendments, and fertilization. Likewise, it is neccessary to understand the growth habits of the plantings selected, as plants with abundant foliar growth may obscure windows or prove too heavy for some modular systems.

## CLOSED WATER SYSTEMS

Both green roofs and vertical gardens usually require the use of drought tolerant plants in order to succeed. Roofs and building perimeters are subject to tough environmental conditions. Recent pressures on water resources have led to restrictions on water for use in irrigation throughout the built environment and a need to find alternative sources of water. Responsive designers have discovered creative means to harvest roof runoff, A/C condensate, and building sewage, treated onsite with UV sterilization or wetland systems to clean the water enough that it can be used to support plant life. Such systems lessen the pressures on our dwindling resources while still supporting all the benefits of green spaces.

In establishing these closed water systems, designers need to consider a number of factors. Recycled water, while cheap and available, is generally of poorer quality than potable water. It tends to contain salts (trace elements such as chlorine, sodium,

and boron), which can injure sensitive plants unless removed by reverse osmosis treatment, and it often has an undesirable pH for plant life. It sometimes, however, contains nutrients, such as nitrogen, phosphorous, and sulfur, that can be advantageous to plant growth. Designers need to consider plant salt tolerance, soil texture, drainage, and irrigation frequency to leach out salts and prevent plant mortality if no further treatment of the water is available. Areas that are best suited to the use of recycled water are turf and meadows, established tree and shrub plantings that require very little supplementary irrigation, and sites with high natural rainfall.

## SENSITIVE MATERIALS SELECTION

One of the key ways designers can achieve sustainable design is in their materials selection. This means not only selecting materials that are acquired or manufactured by sustainable means or are renewable resources, but also asking about their method of transport, the energy and techniques required to process and install them, their longevity and durability, their maintenance requirements, their emissions of VOCs or other pollutants, and the processes for their eventual removal or recycling. Instead of bringing in new materials, designers can consider reusing existing materials in place, reclaiming materials from other sources, or reducing the amount of material needed for design. A number of new "green" products utilize byproducts of manufacturing in innovative ways, and new markets exist today for materials that were formerly considered waste products.

In addition to careful selection of materials used in construction, designers should also be sensitive to plant materials selection. This means not only selecting plants that will survive and thrive in the specific microclimate of the built environment but also increasing species diversity in these environments. Within our urban areas, we have created large expanses of plantings with little to no species diversity. These monocultures are at high risk of devastation by a single pathogen or insect that may become introduced to the area. Likewise, we have introduced exotic plant species into regions where no natural predators exists, and some of these plants have proved invasive and displaced the native species of the region, reducing habitat for organisms that would otherwise thrive there.

## BIOMIMICRY

From the Greek *bios*, meaning life, and *mimesis*, meaning imitation, biomimicry refers to the rather recent rebirth of an age-old practice of taking inspiration from nature—its models, systems, processes, and elements—to solve design problems in a sustainable way. Nature has adapted over millions of years to "manufacture" its materials under biologically friendly conditions: at room temperature, with sunlight and without chemicals, with pressure, and so forth, cre-

ating materials that are much more resilient, more efficient, more durable, stronger, stickier, self-repairing, biodegradable, and so on, than any material a human has ever been able to create. Today, advocates of biomimicry encourage the examination of nature and its systems to solve modern-day design problems and broaden design teams to include ecologists and biologists.

This practice is not new; in early Islamic history, design elements and ornament were based on plant motifs, and designers created patterns from stylized versions of tendrils, leaves, and stalks, although the intent was often aesthetic rather than functional. This trend was revisited during Art Nouveau, when the flowing, organic forms of the botanical world were incorporated into everyday life. We can also see, in the earliest Egyptian tombs, an imitation of nature in the nonstructural fluted columns that were constructed to resemble bundles of reed or papyrus (Fig. 10.10). Many centuries later, during the Greek and Roman empires, this fluted column appeared again, but in structural form, becoming trunklike, yet still aesthetically enhanced with an ornate bud-shaped capital that was frequently carved with acanthus leaves (Fig. 10.11).

This imitation of nature in structural elements of building architecture was popular during the middle of the eleventh century in Europe, during the medieval era. Churches during that time were constructed from masonry materials, and needed to be large in size, with internal structural stability. Architects took cues from their Roman predecessors and created an interior column and vaulting system that resembled forest of trunks and canopies, strong enough to support the roof over wide expanses while also conducive to promoting the acoustics of the church (Fig. 10.12). Capitals, cast in concrete, continued to be decorated with vines, leaves and other plantlike features, further contributing to the effect of a masonry forest.

This architectural trend continued and was further enhanced during the Gothic era (1140–1500 AD), when the forms and spaces became more slender and skeletal in nature, allowing more light to enter into the building. More voids were allowed between these finer structural members and, in a sense, the architects played with the texture of the "forests" of columns and buttresses. During this time, the flying buttress was first employed for both design and function—a structural element that transmited the horizontal thrust of an interior vaulted ceiling through the walls, acting as a counterweight outside the building (Fig. 10.13). While the buttress structure was used in earlier Roman times, it was usually concealed. In nature, tree buttresses provide structural support to maintain the weight of the tree's trunk and canopy. Some trees growing in wet soils have shallow root systems but develop buttress roots in order to accommodate the need for oxygen exchange. Buttress roots are

10.10 Fluted columns mimic bundles of reeds.

10.12 Vaulted ceilings resemble an interior forest of trunks and canopies. (Photo by Adam W. Turner.)

10.11 The capitals of columns are often enhanced with carvings of acanthus leaves. (Photo by Adam W. Turner.)

exposed roots that emerge from the side of the trunk and expand horizontally to provide a broad structural support to help anchor the tree into the soil, while still functioning to obtain water and nutrients for the plant to survive (Fig. 10.14).

Around the turn of the twentieth cen-

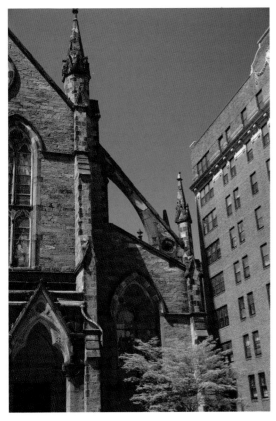

10.13 Flying buttresses mimic buttress roots found in nature. (Photo by Adam W. Turner.)

10.14 Buttress roots provide structural support in wet soils.

tury, a more utopian vision drew artists and designers to provide well-designed environments that allowed people to function to their full potential, and the botanical world continued to influence and inspire these designs. The architect Frank Lloyd Wright was a forerunner during this time, designing buildings that interacted spatially with their natural environment and developing a highly cantilevered style of architecture that was derived from trees (Fig. 10.15). Wright believed that people lived better when nature was easily accessible from their homes, a viewpoint shared by the landscape architect Frederick Law Olmsted, and he adjusted his structures to fit within the landscape.

This trend continues today within the green movement, although further advancements in technology, along with a broader understanding of ecological systems, are allowing us to engineer even more advanced building materials and systems to assist in creating buildings that fit even more seamlessly, from an ecological standpoint, into the landscape. Recent, notable biomimetic products include the following:

10.15 Frank Lloyd Wright's highly cantilevered style of architecture was inspired by trees. He also believed strongly in incorporating architecture into the landscape. (Photo by Marcus Gleysteen.)

- **Composite wood products** (Fig. 10.16): These products mimic natural wood in their appearance. They are comprised of reclaimed wood particles and recycled plastic and therefore produce less waste, are less susceptible to weather changes, are longer lasting, and tend to be cheaper and lower maintenance than their natural counterparts. Composite products such as Azek, TimberTech and Trex, among others, are becoming increasingly more popular as their design becomes more refined and they more closely resemble natural wood in appearance.

- **Water-repellent paint**: These products are inspired by the lotus leaf, which has, in essence, a self-cleaning, nonstick surface that does not allow water, dirt, or microorganisms to adhere to it. During rainfall, tiny droplets of water wash away microscopic particles and clean the leaf. In a similar way, the surfaces of the structures painted with products such as

10.16 Composite products made of reclaimed wood particles and recycled plastic closely resemble natural wood.

Lotusan, Haruna, and Si-Rex03, among others, are kept clean by rainwater.

- **Carbon-sequestering cement**: Approximately 5% of $CO_2$ emissions come from the manufacture of cement—for every ton of cement that is manufactured, a ton of $CO_2$ is released into the atmosphere. Several manufacturers are finding ways to adjust the "recipe" for cement, as well as its production, in order to reverse this process. One such manufacturer, the Calera Corporation, is developing a process that utilizes the $CO_2$ emissions from burning coal that are bubbled through seawater in order to precipitate carbonate minerals for use in cement. Other manufacturers are finding ways to produce cement using alternatives to carbonates, such as titanium dioxide, which chemically reacts, using sunlight, to break down organic pollutants, and magnesium dioxide, which requires carbon dioxide in order to harden. The latter process, developed by TecEco, mimics photosynthesis, in which plants absorb carbon dioxide in order to create sugars.

- **Soy paint**: Several manufacturers have developed eco-friendly paints that replace one or more of the petrochemical-derived components with soy, a renewable and nontoxic (low VOC) material derived from plants. In addition, some manufacturers have substituted the colorants, which are generally chemical-based and toxic, with clay pigments. Green Planet Paints is one such manufacturer that supplies clay-pigment paint with a soy-based resin. This paint also contains titanium dioxide, which assists in odor and pollution absorption, a functionality common also to plants. Sherwin-Williams and EcoProCote also offer soy-based, eco-friendly paints,

- **Photovoltaic skin**: A technology in which solar modules containing semiconductors are secured to the surfaces of buildings to convert a portion of the sun's energy into electricity, much like plants convert solar energy into sugars through photosynthesis. These solar cells are able to operate without emissions or moving parts, and therefore with minimal maintenance or pollution.

## EVOLUTION IN PLANTS AND DESIGN

Plants have existed on earth for millions of years, much longer than humans, and have adapted to their changing environments in awe-inspiring ways. Designers can take cues from these adaptations, and from the process of evolution itself, in order to inform and evaluate their designs.

When Charles Darwin discovered the species of cactus that showed the presence or absence of a stem depending on the presence of a predator, what he discovered was an example of coevolution. Coevolution is the change that occurs within either a subgroup or an entire species that is triggered by the change of a related species (or multiple related species), when each party in the relationship exerts selective pressures on the other, affecting each other's evolution. Coevolution only applies to this process as it involves the pressures from living organisms, as opposed to those exerted by abiotic (non-living) factors such as climate, which often play a role in evolutionary change.

As designers, we can consider the role of coevolution to aid in selection of appropriate plant species for a particular space. For example, many bird and flower species have coevolved over time. If the goal of a design is to attract specific species of wildlife, we can include in the plant palette plant species that have coevolved with that wildlife. Many hummingbirds, for example, have coevolved with orchids, fuchsia, and other flowers with long corollas that allow for the long beaks of the birds to reach the food source, a nectar chemistry that suits the bird's dietary requirements, a flower color that corresponds to the bird's range of vision, and a bloom time that corresponds to the bird's breeding season (Fig. 10.17). Each of the characteristics of the bird and the plant evolved simultaneously.

This example of the hummingbird and the orchid or fuchsia is also one of mutualistic symbiosis, a close interaction between different biological species in which both individuals derive a benefit. In this instance, the hummingbird derives nectar, which provides the bird with necessary energy, and the flower receives a means of pollination. Mycorrhizae and plant roots provide another example of mutualistic symbiosis: the mycorrhizal fungus derives food energy from the plant root and the plant gains a larger root

10.17 Hummingbirds and orchids have coevolved: birds obtain the proper food and flowers are pollinated.

surface area with which to obtain necessary water and nutrients from the soil and assist the plant in survival. In addition to mutualistic forms of symbiosis, two other types of symbiosis occur in nature as well: parasitic symbiosis, when the relationship is detrimental to one of the organisms, and commensal symbiosis, when one of the organisms benefits and the other is not significantly harmed or benefited. Symbiosis is seen as a driving force behind evolution.

Beyond the botanical benefits of coevolution and mutualistic symbiosis, designers can also learn from evolution in other, more abstract ways. Many designers of contemporary architecture have utilized sustainable and defensive building strategies based on years of evolutionary advancements in plants. Architects have taken cues from plants to develop methods of climate control for buildings, using various organic and inorganic building materials to insulate from extremes of temperature, reflect heat or shade, and reduce solar heat. They have used plant forms and structures to control water, redirecting storm water to underground cisterns that can be used to cool buildings, irrigate landscapes, or fill sanitary systems in much the same way that plants adapted to arid climates, such as aloe, use their leaves to funnel water back to the main axis of the plant and into the ground, and roots, below. Some plant forms have also inspired design to ameliorate extreme weather conditions. For example, many conifers have a pyramidal shape to shed snow, reduce weight on branches, and reduce wind load in winter; this shape has been used in buildings in arctic regions. Architects can also learn from some of the natural defense strategies plants have adopted. For example, buildings requiring higher levels of security have been designed with spinelike or other defensive structures to prevent vehicles and pedestrians from getting too close. (More examples can be found in Bahamon, Perez, and Campello, 2006; see References). Engineers, too, have taken cues from plant adaptations. A new product has recently been invented at the Beckman Institute at the University of Illinois, Urbana, that mimics plants' natural defense in response to pruning. A self-healing polymer, composed of structural polymeric material and a catalytic chemical trigger, has the ability to automatically repair cracks and reduce or eliminate the need to replace the polymer once it is compromised. These polymers have potential applications for objects from industrial equipment to building facades to laptops.

Perhaps the most useful lesson designers can learn from the botanical world is the fact that plants are continuously adapting to their environments. Nature is ever changing, and the only way organisms can survive is to respond to challenges and be resilient to change. Designers can imitate this evolutionary process by creating designs that can be adapted as the needs of the user, as well as the pressures of the site, change, rather than copying preexisting prototypes or creating fixed spaces. Buildings and landscapes that have become dilapidated, deserted, or obsolete often have deteriorated because they were not designed to adapt and conform to the changing pressures of the user and the environment. When buildings outlive their original use, they may be left vacant, or renovated at significant environmental and financial cost. As designers, we can help develop a better process. With a careful study of the past and the present of our design sites, we can anticipate future needs and create interior and exterior environments that are amenable to change. In the end, the best survival strategy for designed environments is much the same as that of the biological world: to be adaptable and resilient.

11.1 Appropriate plant selection ensures the health and vibrancy of our landscapes.

# EPILOGUE: FURTHER EXPLORATIONS

Designers are busy practitioners, often working on tight deadlines in order to respond to client needs. As a result, we may find few opportunities outside the workday—which often extends late into the night and over the weekend—to expand our knowledge base. Often, our only introductions to new plant varieties and cultivars are made while flipping through magazines during a quick lunch break, and we likely have not had the opportunity to study *why* plants are able to provide us with so much comfort and enjoyment. It is my hope that this book will serve as a base for a new exploration of botany, inspiring us take a different view of plants as we journey through the landscape during our daily routines (Fig. 11.1).

The next time you visit a garden or other landscaped space, ask new questions: How are these plants surviving? Are they being maintained appropriately? How could the main-

tenance plan be better? Has soil compaction caused damage, and if so, what is the source of the compaction and how could it have been prevented? Are there signs of other types of damage or plant vulnerability, and if so, what has caused it and how could it have been avoided? Is this landscape aging well? Has the design intent been maintained? What are the most pleasing plant features of this landscape, and why? Asking ourselves these questions will help us make better informed planting decisions in our future designs.

While perusing magazines and nursery catalogs is a quick way to learn a few new varieties and cultivars, I encourage every designer to make a visit to a local nursery, on a seasonal basis if possible. Ask the nursery manager what the latest introductions are and why they are better. Do they have better tolerances to particular pests? Do they have superior cold resistance? A different habit or flower color? Perhaps a new introduction can inspire a new planting design.

Trade shows are another good way to learn about the latest technological advances in landscape design and construction. They often provide information about new products such as root barriers, biostimulants, lumber selections, planters, irrigation systems, and other products that can assist in solving problems in the landscape with a sustainable approach.

Our increased understanding of botany—from plant nomenclature to morphology to functionality to cultural requirements—can assist us in choosing appropriate plant species and cultivars and ensuring the long-term health and vibrancy of our plantings. As we apply cues from nature to our built environments, we can not only slow the degeneration of ecosystem health and the depletion of natural resources, but also participate in the opportunity to become stewards of our land and our landscapes, maintaining and improving ecological health in order to secure the future of the environment. These lessons can come from plants.

# APPENDIX A:
# COMMON BOTANICAL TERMS USED IN HORTICULTURE

Below is a list of common botanical terms, primarily derived from Latin and Greek, which I have accumulated over many years from various sources (texts, websites, etc.). This list is by no means exhaustive, but is a starting point meant to give designers an indication of the type of design information that can be gleaned from the scientific names given to plants.

abyssinica: from Abysinnia (Ethiopia)
acaulis: without a stem
aculeatus: prickly, thorny
acuminatus: tapering to a long point
acutifolius: with sharp leaves
aestivalis: summer-flowering
aggregatus: clustered
alatus: winged
albus: white
alpestris: alpine
alpinus: alpine

altissimus: tallest
amabilis: beautiful
americana: from America
angularis: angular
angustifolius: with narrow leaves
annuus: annual
arborescens: tree-like
argenteus: silvery
arvensis: of the field
asteriasis: star-like
atropurpureus dark purple
aureus: golden
auriculatus: eared
autumnalis: flowering in autumn
azureus: azure
borealis: from the North
caeruleus: blue
campanulatus: bell-shaped
campestris: found in plains
canadensis: from Canad
candidus: white

chinensis: from Chin
coccineus: scarlet
coeruleus: sky-blue
colosseus: gigantic
columnaris: columnar
compactus: compact
contortus: twisted
cordatus: heart-shaped
cuspidatus: ending in a sharp, stiff point
densiflorus: with dense flowers
dentatus: toothed
digitata: like a hand
dissectus: deeply cut
divaricatus: widely spreading
divergens: divergent
elatus: tall
elegans: elegant
elongatus: elongated
erectus: erect
farinosa: floury, powdery
filicifolius: with fern-like leaves
filifolius: with thread-like leaves
fistulosus: tubular
flavulus: yellow
flavus: yellow
floribundus: free-flowering
floriferus: flower-bearing
fragrans: sweet-scented
frutescens: shrubby
fulvus: reddish-yellow
giganteus: huge
glaber: smooth
glaucus: covered with a greyish bloom
globosus: spherical
glutinosus: sticky
gracilis: graceful
grandiflorus: with large flowers

grandis: large
helianthus: sun-flower
herbaceus: herbaceous, not woody
hirsutus: hairy
hirtus: hairy
hispidus: bristly
humilis: low-growing
incisifolius: with cut leaves
inermis: unarmed, without spines
inodorus: scentless
laetus: vivid
laevigatus: smooth
laevis: smooth
lanatus: woolly
lanceolatus: lance-shaped
latifolia: wide-leaved
leucanthus: with white flowers
lucidus: shining
luteus: yellow
macrocarpus: with large fruit
macrophyllus: with large leaves
maculatus: spotted
maritimus: found growing on the coast
maximus: largest
micropetalus: with small petals
mollis: soft
nanus: dwarf
niger: black
nocturnalis: night-flowering
occidentalis: western
oculatus: with an eye
odoratus: fragrant
officinalis: used medicinally
orbicularis: round
orientalis: eastern
palmatus: lobed like a hand
palustris: found growing in swampy places

paniculatus: paniculate

parviflorus: with small flowers

pendulus: drooping, hanging

petiolaris: with stalked leaves

plumosus: feathery

praecox: early flowering

procumbens: lying along the ground

pubescens: covered with downy hairs

pumilus: dwarf

pungens: sharp-pointed, pricking

purpureus: purple

pygmaeus: dwarf

pyramidalis: pyramidal

racemosus: with flowers borne in racemes

reticulatus: covered with a network of veins

roseus: rose-colored

ruber: red

rugosus: wrinkled

sanguineus: blood-red

scandens: climbing

semperflorens: ever-flowering

sempervirens: evergreen

serotinus: produced late in the season

serratus: saw-toothed

serrulatus: somewhat saw-toothed

sinuatus: with a wavy margin

speciosus: showy

spectabilis: spectacular

spinosus: spiny

splendens: splendid

stellatus: with spreading, star-like rays

sterilis: sterile

strictus: erect

succulentus: fleshy

superbus: superb

sylvaticus: found growing in woods

sylvestris: found wild

tenuifolius: with slender leaves

tigrinus: striped like a tiger

tinctorius: used in dyeing

tomentosus: covered with fine, matted hairs

trilobatus: three-lobed

tripteris: three-winged

tuberosus: tuberous

undulatus: wavy

urens: stinging

variabilis: variable

variegatus: variegated

vernalis: flowering in spring

versicolor: changing color

verticillatus: whorled

virens: green

vulgaris: common

zebrinus: zebra-striped

# APPENDIX B: PLANT PALETTES

Below are lists of some of my plant favorites, arranged by design characteristics and cultural requirements. These plants have been reliable choices for me in zone 6. Not meant to be exhaustive, these recommendations are provided as a starting point for designers.

## PLANTS FOR DIFFERENT GROWTH HABITS

### PROSTRATE (CREEPING AND SPREADING)

*Arctostaphylos uva-ursi* (bearberry): zone 3, 6–12" ht. evergreen groundcover, sun to part shade

*Calluna vulgaris* (heather): zone 5, 4–24" ht. evergreen shrub, full sun to part shade

*Cotoneaster horizontalis* (rockspray cotoneaster): zone 4, 2–3' ht. deciduous shrub, sun to part shade

*Forsythia* 'Courtasol' (gold tide forsythia): zone 5, 1–2' ht. deciduous shrub, full sun

*Geranium* sp. (cranesbill): zone 3, 6–18" ht. perennial, sun to part shade

*Hedera helix* (English ivy): zone 5, 6–8" ht. evergreen groundcover, sun to shade

*Juniperus horizontalis* 'Bar Harbor' (Bar Harbor juniper): zone 3, 6–8" ht. evergreen shrub, full sun

*Liriope spicata* (lilyturf): zone 4, 8–12" semi–evergreen groundcover, sun to shade

*Phlox subulata* (ground phlox): zone 3, 3–6" ht. perennial, sun to part shade

*Stephanandra incisa* 'Crispa' (cutleaf stephanandra): zone 4, 18–36" ht. deciduous shrub, sun to part shade

*Vaccinium angustifolium* (lowbush blueberry): zone 2, 6–18" ht. deciduous shrub, sun to part shade

*Vinca minor* (periwinkle): zone 4, 4–8" ht. evergreen groundcover, shade to part sun

## OVAL TO ROUNDED

*Acer rubrum* (red maple): zone 3, 40–50' ht. deciduous tree, full sun

*Acer saccharum* (sugar maple): zone 3, 60–75' ht. deciduous tree, sun to part shade

*Caryopteris* x *clandonensis (blue mist spirea)*: zone 5, 2–3' ht. deciduous shrub, full sun

*Coreopsis verticillata* (tickseed): zone 4, 14–24" ht. perennial, sun to part shade

*Daphne* x *burkwoodii* (daphne): zone 5, 3–4' ht. semi–evergreen shrub, sun to part shade

*Hydrangea macrophylla* (hydrangea): zone 6, 3–5' ht. deciduous shrub, sun to part shade

*Malus* sp. (flowering crabapple): zone 4, 8–30' ht. deciduous tree, full sun

*Rhododendron* sp. (azalea): variable zones, 2–6' ht. deciduous or evergreen shrub, sun to part shade

*Rhododendron* sp. (rhododendron): variable zones, 3–12' ht. evergreen shrub, part shade

*Tilia cordata* (littleleaf linden): zone 3, 40–50' ht. deciduous tree, sun to part shade

## FASTIGIATE, UPRIGHT, CONICAL, OR PYRAMIDAL

*Abies concolor* (white fir): zone 4, 30–50' ht. evergreen tree, full sun

*Acer rubrum* 'Armstrong' (Armstrong red maple): zone 3, 50–70' ht. deciduous tree, full sun

*Carpinus betulus* 'Fastigiata' (pyramidal European hornbeam): zone 5, 30–40' ht. deciduous tree, sun to part shade

*Delphinium* x *elatum* (delphinium): zone 3, 3' ht. perennial, full sun

*Digitalis purpurea* (foxglove): zone 4, 24–48" ht. perennial, sun to part shade

*Fagus sylvatica* 'Fastigiata' (upright European beech): zone 5, 50–60' ht. deciduous tree, full sun

*Gleditsia triacanthos* 'Skyline' (Skyline honeylocust): zone 4, 30–50' ht. deciduous tree, full sun

*Ilex crenata* 'Sky Pencil' (Sky Pencil holly): zone 6, 6–8' ht. evergreen shrub, sun to part shade

*Ilex* x *meserveae* (Meserve holly): zone 5, 6–10' ht. evergreen shrub, sun to shade

*Iris sibirica* (Siberian iris): zone 3, 24–36" ht. perennial, sun to part shade

*Juniperus chinensis* 'Hetzii Columnaris' (Hetz columnar juniper): zone 4, 10–15' ht. evergreen shrub, full sun

*Liriodendron tulipifera* (tuliptree): zone 5, 70–90' ht. deciduous tree, full sun

*Metasequoia glyptostroboides* (dawn redwood): zone 4, 60–90', full sun

*Picea pungens* (Colorado spruce): zone 3, 30–60' ht. evergreen tree, full sun

*Pseudotsuga menziesii* (douglasfir): zone 4, 40–50' ht. evergreen tree, full sun

*Quercus palustris* (pin oak): zone 4, 60–70' ht. deciduous tree, full sun

*Quercus robur* 'Fastigiata' (upright English

oak): zone 4, 50–60' ht. deciduous tree, full sun

*Salvia nemorosa* (meadow sage): zone 4, 14–24" ht. perennial, full sun

*Taxus* x *media* 'Hicksii' (Hicks upright yew): zone 4, 6–10' ht. evergreen shrub, sun to shade

## HORIZONTAL

*Acer palmatum* (Japanese maple): zone 5, 5–20' ht. deciduous tree, sun to part shade

*Achillea millefolium* (yarrow): zone 3, 15–24" ht. perennial, full sun

*Chamaecyparis obtusa* 'Gracilis' (Hinoki cypress): zone 5, 9–15' ht. evergreen tree, full sun

*Cornus kousa* (kousa dogwood): zone 5, 20–25' ht. deciduous tree, sun to part shade

*Hydrangea macrophylla* 'Mariesii' (lacecap hydrangea): zone 6, 3–5' ht. deciduous shrub, sun to part shade

*Sedum spectabile* 'Autumn Joy' (Autumn Joy stonecrop): zone 3, 2–36" ht. perennial, full sun

*Viburnum plicatum* var. *tomentosum* (doublefile viburnum): zone 5, 5–10' ht. deciduous shrub, sun to part shade

## IRREGULAR

*Corylus avellana* 'Contorta' (Harry Lauder's walking stick): zone 3, 8–10' ht. deciduous shrub, full sun

## WEEPING

*Betula pendula* (weeping birch): zone 2, 20–25' ht. deciduous tree, full sun

*Cedrus atlantica* 'Glauca Pendula' (weeping Blue Atlas cedar): zone 6, 10–18' ht. evergreen tree, full sun

*Chamaecyparis nootkatensis* 'Pendula' (weeping Alaska cedar): zone 4, 15–25' ht. evergreen tree, full sun to part shade

*Fagus sylvatica* 'Pendula' (weeping European beech): zone 5, 50–60' ht. deciduous tree, full sun

*Morus alba* 'Pendula' (weeping mulberry): zone 4, 15–20' ht. deciduous tree, full sun

*Picea abies* 'Pendula' (weeping Norway spruce): zone 3, 12–20' ht. evergreen tree, full sun

*Prunus subhirtella* 'Pendula' (weeping cherry): zone 5, 15–18' ht. deciduous tree, full sun

*Salix alba* 'Tristis' (golden weeping willow): zone 2, 30–40' ht. deciduous tree, full sun

# STREET TREES

*Acer rubrum* 'October Glory' (October Glory red maple): zone 3, 40–50' ht. deciduous tree, full sun

*Carpinus betulus* (European hornbeam): zone 5, 40–60' ht. deciduous tree, sun to part shade

*Fraxinus americana* 'Junginger' (Autumn Purple ash): zone 4, 50–60' ht. deciduous tree, full sun

*Fraxinus pennsylvanica* 'Marshall's Seedless' (green ash): zone 3, 50–60' ht. deciduous tree, full sun

*Ginkgo biloba* (ginkgo): zone 4, 50–80' ht. deciduous tree, full sun

*Gleditsia triacanthos* 'Shademaster' (Shademaster honeylocust): zone 4, 30–50' ht. deciduous tree, full sun

*Platanus* x *acerifolia* (London planetree): zone 5, 40–50' ht. deciduous tree, sun to part shade

*Quercus rubra* (red oak): zone 3, 60–70' ht. deciduous tree, full sun

*Tilia cordata* 'Greenspire' (Greenspire littleleaf linden): zone 3, 40–50' ht. deciduous tree, full sun

*Ulmus americana* 'Valley Forge' (American elm): zone 5, 50–70' ht. deciduous tree, full sun

*Zelkova serrata* (zelkova): zone 5, 35–50' ht. deciduous tree, sun to part shade

## PLANTS FOR HEDGES

*Acer campestre* (hedge maple): zone 4, 25–35' ht. deciduous tree, sun to part shade

*Buxus* sp. (boxwood): zone 5, 2–10' ht. evergreen shrub, full sun

*Carpinus betulus* (European hornbeam): zone 5, 40–60' ht. deciduous tree, sun to part shade

*Crataegus crusgalli* var. *inermis* (thornless cockspur hawthorn): zone 4, 20–30' ht. deciduous tree, full sun

*Ilex crenata* (Japanese holly): zone 6, 3–8' ht. evergreen shrub, sun to part shade

*Ilex glabra* (inkberry): zone 5, 3–6' ht. evergreen shrub, sun to shade

*Lavandula angustifolia* (lavender): zone 5, 12–30" ht. perennial, full sun

*Ligustrum* sp. (privet): zone 4, 5–12' ht. semi–evergreen shrub, sun to shade

*Pyracantha coccinea* (firethorn): zone 6, 6–12' ht. semi–evergreen shrub, sun to part shade

*Rosa rugosa* (rugosa rose): zone 2, 4–6' ht. deciduous shrub, full sun

*Spiraea* x *vanhouttei* (vanhoutte spirea): zone 4, 6–8' ht. deciduous shrub, full sun

*Syringa meyeri* 'Palibin' (dwarf Korean lilac): zone 3, 4–5' ht. deciduous shrub, full sun

*Taxus* sp. (yew): zone 4, 2–20' ht. evergreen shrub, sun to shade

*Thuja occidentalis* (eastern arborvitae): zone 3, 4–25' ht. evergreen shrub, full sun

*Viburnum trilobum* (American cranberrybush): zone 2, 5–12' ht. deciduous shrub, sun to part shade

## PLANTS FOR TEXTURE

### FINE TEXTURE

*Acer palmatum dissectum* 'Tamukeyama' (Tamukeyama threadleaf Japanese maple): zone 5, 8–10' ht. deciduous tree, sun to part shade

*Betula pendula* (weeping birch): zone 2, 20–25' ht. deciduous tree, full sun

*Buxus* sp. (boxwood): zone 5, 2–10' ht. evergreen shrub, full sun

*Caryopteris* x *clandonensis* (blue mist spirea): zone 5, 2–3' ht. deciduous shrub, full sun

*Chamaecyparis pisifera* 'Filifera' (threadleaf cypress): zone 4, 12–20' ht. evergreen shrub, sun to part shade

*Coreopsis verticillata* (tickseed): zone 4, 14–24" ht. perennial, sun to part shade

*Deutzia gracilis* (slender deutzia): zone 5, 3–5' ht. deciduous shrub, full sun

*Gleditsia triacanthos* (honeylocust): zone 4, 30–50' ht. deciduous tree, full sun

*Ilex crenata* (Japanese holly): zone 6, 3–8' ht. evergreen shrub, sun to part shade

*Ilex glabra* (inkberry): zone 5, 3–6' ht. evergreen shrub, sun to shade

*Kerria japonica* (Japanese kerria): zone 5, 3–6' ht. deciduous shrub, shade

*Osmunda cinnamomea* (cinnamon fern): zone 3, 36–60" ht. perennial, shade

*Potentilla fruticosa* (potentilla): zone 2, 2–3' ht. deciduous shrub, sun to part shade

*Salix integra* 'Hakuro Nishiki' (dappled willow): zone 5, 5–8' ht. deciduous shrub, full sun

*Spiraea* sp. (spirea): zone 4, 2–8' ht. deciduous shrub, full sun

## COARSE TEXTURE

*Acer saccharum* (sugar maple): zone 3, 60–75' ht. deciduous tree, sun to part shade

*Aesculus hippocastanum* (horsechestnut): zone 3, 50–75' ht. deciduous tree, full sun

*Catalpa speciosa* (northern catalpa): zone 4, 40–70' ht. deciduous tree, sun to part shade

*Cercis canadensis* (eastern redbud): zone 4, 20–30' ht. deciduous tree, sun to part shade

*Echinacea purpurea* (coneflower): zone 3, 18–36" ht. perennial, full sun

*Fothergilla major* (fothergilla): zone 5, 6–10' ht. deciduous shrub, sun to part shade

*Hamamelis* x *intermedia* 'Arnold Promise' (Arnold Promise witchhazel): zone 4, 10–15' ht. deciduous shrub, sun to part shade

*Hemerocallis* sp. (daylily): zone 3, 10–36" ht. perennial, sun to part shade

*Hosta* sp. (plantain lily): zone 3, 12–36" ht. perennial, part sun to shade

*Hydrangea macrophylla* (hydrangea): zone 6, 3–5' ht. deciduous shrub, sun to part shade

*Leucanthemum* x *superbum* (shasta daisy): zone 5, 12–36" ht. perennial, sun to part shade

*Magnolia* x *soulangiana* (saucer magnolia): zone 6, 20–30' ht. deciduous tree, full sun

*Mahonia aquifolium* (Oregon grape holly): zone 5, 3–6' ht. evergreen shrub, shade

*Platanus* x *acerifolia* (London planetree): zone 5, 40–50' ht. deciduous tree, sun to part shade

*Rhododendron* sp. (rhododendron): variable zones, 3–12' ht. evergreen shrub, part shade

# PLANTS FOR COLORFUL FOLIAGE

## RED

*Acer palmatum* 'Bloodgood' (Bloodgood Japanese maple): zone 5, 15–18' ht. deciduous tree, sun to part shade

*Athyrium nipponicum* 'Pictum' (Japanese painted fern): zone 4, 12–24" ht. perennial, shade

*Cercis canadensis* 'Forest Pansy' (Forest Pansy redbud): zone 4, 15–20' ht. deciduous tree, sun to part shade

*Cotinus coggygria* 'Royal Purple' (Royal Purple smoketree): zone 5, 8–10' ht. deciduous shrub, full sun

*Fagus sylvatica* 'Purple Fountain' (Purple Fountain European beech): zone 5, 30–40' ht. deciduous tree, full sun

*Heuchera* x 'Plum Pudding' (coralbells): zone 3, 10–24" ht. perennial, sun to part shade

*Malus* 'Prairifire' (Prairifire flowering crab): zone 4, 15–20' ht. deciduous tree, full sun

*Physocarpus opulifolius* 'Diablo' (common ninebark): zone 2, 5–10' ht. deciduous shrub, sun to part shade

*Prunus cerasifera* 'Thundercloud' (purpleleaf plum): zone 3, 15–20' ht. deciduous tree, full sun

*Weigela florida* 'Alexandra' (Wine and Roses weigela): zone 5, 4–5' ht. deciduous shrub, full sun

## YELLOW

*Acer palmatum* var. *dissectum* 'Flavescens' (Japanese maple): zone 5, 6–8' ht. deciduous tree, sun to part shade

*Chamaecyparis pisifera* 'Filifera Aurea' (golden threadleaf cypress): zone 4, 6–15' ht. evergreen shrub, sun to part shade

*Gleditsia triacanthos* 'Sunburst' (Sunburst honeylocust): zone 4, 30–50' ht. deciduous tree, full sun

*Hakonechloa macra* 'Areola' (golden Japanese forest grass): zone 6, 1–2' ht. perennial, part shade

*Juniperus chinensis* 'Gold Lace' (Gold Lace juniper): zone 4, 4–6' ht. evergreen shrub, full sun

*Sedum reflexum* 'Angelina' (stonecrop): zone 3, 3–6" ht. perennial, full sun

*Spiraea japonica* 'Gold Mound' (Gold Mound spirea): zone 4, 2–3' ht. deciduous shrub, full sun

## GRAY/SILVER/BLUE

*Abies concolor* (white fir): zone 4, 30–50' ht. evergreen tree, full sun

*Acer saccharinum* (silver maple): zone 3, 50–70' ht. deciduous tree, sun to part shade

*Artemisia schmidtiana* 'Silver Mound' (wormwood): zone 3, 8–15" ht. perennial, full sun

*Brunnera macrophylla* 'Jack Frost' (brunnera): zone 3, 10–18" ht. perennial, shade

*Caryopteris* x *clandonensis* (blue mist spirea): zone 5, 2–3' ht. deciduous shrub, full sun

*Cedrus atlantica* 'Glauca' (Blue Atlas cedar): zone 6, 15–25' ht. evergreen tree, full sun

*Cerastium tomentosum* (snow-in-summer): zone 3, 4–12" ht. perennial, full sun

*Hosta* 'True Blue' (True Blue plantain lily): zone 3, 12" ht. perennial, part sun to shade

*Juniperus virginiana* 'Gray Owl' (Gray Owl juniper): zone 4, 2–4' ht. evergreen shrub, full sun

*Lavandula angustifolia* (lavender): zone 5, 12–30" ht. perennial, full sun

*Miscanthus sinensis* 'Adagio' (Adagio dwarf silver grass): zone 7, 3–5' ht. perennial, full sun

*Perovskia atriplicifolia* (Russian sage): zone 4, 3–4' ht. perennial, sun to part shade

*Picea pungens* var. *glauca* (Colorado blue spruce): zone 3, 30–60' ht. evergreen tree, full sun

*Populus alba* (white poplar): zone 3, 40–70' ht. deciduous tree, full sun

*Tilia tomentosa* (silver linden): zone 4, 50–70' ht. deciduous tree, full sun

## WHITE OR YELLOW VARIEGATION

*Cornus alba* 'Baihalo' (Ivory Halo tatarian dogwood): zone 4, 4–6' ht. deciduous shrub, sun to part shade

*Daphne* x *burkwoodii* 'Carol Mackie' (Carol Mackie daphne): zone 5, 3–4' ht. semi-evergreen shrub, sun to part shade

*Euonymus fortunei* 'Emerald Gaiety' (Emerald Gaiety euonymus): zone 5, 3–4' ht. evergreen shrub, full sun to part shade

*Euonymus fortunei* 'Emerald 'n Gold' (Emerald 'n Gold euonymus): zone 5, 3–4' ht. evergreen shrub, full sun to part shade

*Hakonechloa macra* 'Aureola' (golden hakone grass): zone 5, 12–18" ht. perennial, part shade

*Hosta* 'Francee' (plantain lily): zone 3, 20–26" ht. perennial, part sun to shade

*Hydrangea macrophylla* 'Mariesii Variegata' (lacecap hydrangea): zone 6, 3–5' ht. deciduous shrub, sun to part shade

*Iris ensata* 'Variegata' (Japanese iris): zone 4, 18–20" ht. perennial, sun to part shade

*Pieris japonica* 'Flaming Silver' (Flaming Silver Japanese andromeda): zone 5, 6–8' ht. evergreen shrub, sun to part shade

*Salix integra* 'Hakuro Nishiki' (dappled willow): zone 5, 5–8' ht. deciduous shrub, full sun

## GOOD FALL COLOR

*Acer rubrum* (red maple): zone 3, red, 40–50' ht. deciduous tree, full sun

*Acer saccharum* (sugar maple): zone 3, yellow-orange, 60–75' ht. deciduous tree, sun to part shade

*Amelanchier canadensis* (serviceberry): zone 3, orange to red, 15–25' ht. deciduous tree, sun to part shade

*Betula* sp. (birch): zone 2, yellow, 20–60' ht. deciduous tree, full sun

*Cercidiphyllum japonicum* (katsuratree): zone 4, yellow-apricot, 40–60' ht. deciduous tree, full sun

*Clethra alnifolia* (summersweet): zone 3, yellow, 4–8' ht. deciduous shrub, sun to shade

*Cornus florida* (flowering dogwood): zone 4, red-purple, 20–25' ht. deciduous tree, sun to part shade

*Cornus kousa* (kousa dogwood): zone 5, red, 20–25' ht. deciduous tree, sun to part shade

*Enkianthus campanulatus* (redvein enkianthus): zone 4, red-orange-yellow, 6–10' ht. deciduous shrub, sun to part shade

*Fothergilla gardenii* (dwarf fothergilla): zone 5, yellow-orange-red, 2–4' ht. deciduous shrub, sun to part shade

*Fraxinus americana* 'Junginger' (Autumn Purple ash): zone 4, deep purple, 50–60' ht. deciduous tree, full sun

*Itea virginica* (sweetspire): zone 6, red-purple, 4–6' ht. deciduous shrub, sun to shade

*Leucothoe fontanesiana* (leucothoe): zone 4, wine red, 3–6' ht. evergreen shrub, part sun to shade

*Liquidambar styraciflua* (sweetgum): zone 5, red-purple-yellow, 60–75' ht. deciduous tree, full sun

*Nyssa sylvatica* (black tupelo): zone 4, red-yellow-purple, 30–50' ht. deciduous tree, sun to part shade

*Oxydendrum arboreum* (sourwood): zone 5, yellow-red-purple, 25–30' ht. deciduous tree, sun to part shade

*Parthenocissus quinquefolia* (Virginia creeper): zone 4, red-purple, 30–50' ht. deciduous vine, sun to shade

*Stewartia pseudocamellia* (Japanese stewartia): zone 6, yellow-red-purple, 20–40' ht. deciduous tree, full sun

*Vaccinium corymbosum* (highbush blueberry): zone 3, red-orange-purple-yellow, 4–8' ht. deciduous shrub, sun to part shade

*Viburnum trilobum* (American cranberrybush): zone 2, red-purple, 5–12' ht. deciduous shrub, sun to part shade

## PLANTS FOR FRAGRANCE

*Abeliophyllum distichum* (white forsythia): zone 5, fragrant flowers, 4–5' ht. deciduous shrub, full sun to part shade

*Abies concolor* (white fir): zone 4, fragrant needles, 30–50' ht. evergreen tree, full sun

*Buddleia davidii* (butterfly bush): zone 5, fragrant flowers, 3–5' ht. deciduous shrub, full sun

*Buxus* sp. (boxwood): zone 5, fragrant foliage and flowers (some find offensive), 2–10' ht. evergreen shrub, full sun

*Calycanthus floridus* (sweetshrub): zone 4, fragrant flowers and stem, 6–9' ht. deciduous shrub, sun or shade

*Caryopteris* x *clandonensis* (blue mist spirea): zone 5, fragrant foliage, 2–3' ht. deciduous shrub, full sun

*Cercidiphyllum japonicum* (katsuratree):

zone 4, fragrant fall foliage, 40–60' ht. deciduous tree, full sun

*Clematis terniflora* (sweet autumn clematis): zone 5, fragrant flowers, 10–20' ht. deciduous vine, sun to part shade

*Clethra alnifolia* (summersweet): zone 3, fragrant flowers, 4–8' ht. deciduous shrub, sun to shade

*Comptonia peregrina* (sweet fern): zone 2, fragrant foliage, 2–3' ht. deciduous shrub, shade

*Convallaria majalis* (lily-of-the-valley): zone 2, fragrant flowers, 6" ht. perennial, shade

*Corylopsis glabrescens* (fragrant winterhazel): zone 5, fragrant flowers, 8–15' ht. deciduous shrub, full sun

*Daphne* x *burkwoodii* 'Carol Mackie' (Carol Mackie daphne): zone 5, fragrant flowers, 3–4' ht. semi-evergreen shrub, sun to part shade

*Fothergilla gardenii* (dwarf fothergilla): zone 5, fragrant flowers, 2–4' ht. deciduous shrub, sun to part shade

*Itea virginica* (sweetspire): zone 6, fragrant flowers, 4–6' ht. deciduous shrub, sun to shade

*Lavandula angustifolia* (lavender): zone 5, fragrant flowers and foliage, 12–30" ht. perennial, full sun

*Magnolia virginiana* (sweetbay magnolia): zone 5, fragrant flowers, 10–20' ht. deciduous tree, sun to part shade

*Myrica pensylvanica* (northern bayberry): zone 2, fragrant foliage, 6–10' ht. semi-evergreen shrub, sun to part shade

*Paeonia* sp. (peony): zone 4, fragrant flowers (some cultivars), 36–60" ht. perennial or shrub, sun to part shade

*Philadelphus coronarius* (mockorange): zone 4, fragrant flowers, 8–10' ht. deciduous shrub, full sun

*Rhododendron viscosum* (swamp azalea): zone 4, fragrant flowers, 4–8' ht. deciduous shrub, sun to part shade

*Rhus aromatica* 'Gro-low' (Gro-low sumac): zone 3, fragrant foliage, 2' ht. deciduous shrub, full sun

*Rosa* sp. (rose): variable zones, fragrant flowers (some species and cultivars), 2–6' ht. deciduous shrub, full sun

*Sarcococca ruscifolia* (fragrant sarcococca): zone 7, fragrant flowers, 3' ht. evergreen shrub, shade

*Syringa* sp. (lilac): zone 3–5, fragrant flowers, 4–15' ht. deciduous shrub, full sun

*Tilia cordata* (littleleaf linden): zone 3, fragrant flowers, 40–50' ht. deciduous tree, sun to part shade

*Viburnum* x *burkwoodii* (burkwood viburnum): zone 5, fragrant flowers, 8–10' ht. deciduous shrub, sun to part shade

## PLANTS FOR BLOOM TIME

The following is a sample list of striking flowers—woody plants and perennials—that bloom during the listed times in zone 6.

### MARCH

*Abeliophyllum* (white), *Acer rubrum* (red), *Azalea* (purple, pink and white),

*Cornus mas* (yellow), *Erica* (red and pink), *Hamamelis* (yellow, red), *Helleborus* (white, pink, purple), *Magnolia* (white, pink), *Rhododendron* (purple, pink, red, white), *Salix* (yellow), *Sarcococca* (white)

## APRIL

*Amelanchier* (white), *Azalea* (red, pink, white, purple, yellow), *Brunnera* (blue), *Cercis* (purple), *Chaenomeles* (red, orange, pink, white), *Euphorbia* (yellow), *Forsythia* (yellow), *Fothergilla* (white), *Helleborus* (white, pink, purple), *Magnolia* (white, pink), *Mahonia* (yellow), *Malus* (red, pink, white, purple), *Phlox stolonifera* (white, pink, purple), *Pieris* (white), *Prunus* (white, pink, red), *Pulmonaria* (pink, blue), *Pyrus* (white), *Rhododendron* (purple, pink, red, white), *Spiraea* (white, pink)

## MAY

*Amelanchier* (white), *Aquilegia* (red, pink, white, purple, blue), *Aruncus* (cream), *Azalea* (red, pink, white, purple, yellow), *Baptisia* (purple), *Brunnera* (blue), *Chionanthus* (white), *Convallaria* (white), *Cornus florida* (white, pink), *Daphne* (pink, white), *Deutzia* (white), *Dicentra* (pink, white), *Enkianthus* (pink, white), *Euphorbia* (yellow), *Fothergilla* (white), *Geum* (orange), *Halesia* (white), *Heuchera* (pink, purple, white), *Iris* (purple, blue, white, yellow), *Laburnum* (yellow), *Mahonia* (yellow), *Malus* (red, pink, white, purple), *Paeonia* (pink, white, red, purple, yellow), *Papaver* (red,

pink, yellow, orange, white), *Phlox stolonifera* (white, pink, purple), *Potentilla* (yellow), *Prunus* (white, pink, red), *Pulmonaria* (pink, blue), *Pyrus* (white), *Rhododendron* (purple, pink, red, white), *Spiraea* (white, pink), *Syringa* (pink, blue, white, purple), *Viburnum* (white), *Weigela* (red, pink, white), *Wisteria* (purple, white and blue),

## JUNE

*Achillea* (yellow, orange, pink, white), *Alcea* (red, pink, purple, white, yellow), *Aquilegia* (red, pink, white, purple, blue), *Aruncus* (cream), *Asclepias* (orange), *Astilbe* (red, pink, white, purple), *Azalea* (red, pink, white, purple, yellow), *Baptisia* (purple), *Brunnera* (blue), *Campanula* (blue, purple, white), *Clematis* (red, purple, blue, white, pink), *Coreopsis* (yellow, pink), *Cornus kousa* (white), *Cytisus* (yellow), *Delphinium* (blue, pink, purple, white), *Dicentra* (pink, white), *Digitalis* (pink, white, yellow), *Gaura* (pink, white), *Geranium* (blue, purple, pink, white), *Geum* (orange), *Hemerocallis* (yellow, orange, red, pink), *Heuchera* (pink, purple, white), *Iris* (purple, blue, white, yellow), *Itea* (white), *Kalmia* (pink, white), *Lavandula* (purple, pink), *Leucanthemum* (white), *Lupinus* (white, red, pink, yellow, blue, purple), *Nepeta* (blue, purple), *Paeonia* (pink, white, red, purple, yellow), *Papaver* (red, pink, yellow, orange, white), *Philadelphus* (white), *Potentilla* (yellow), *Rosa* (white, yellow, red, pink, purple), *Salvia* (blue, purple, white), *Spiraea* (white, pink), *Stewartia* (white), *Weigela* (red, pink, white)

## JULY

*Achillea* (yellow, orange, pink, white), *Alcea* (red, pink, purple, white, yellow), *Asclepias* (orange), *Astilbe* (red, pink, white, purple), *Buddleia* (white, pink, purple, blue), *Calluna* (red, pink, purple, white), *Campanula* (blue, purple, white), *Campsis* (red), *Caryopteris* (blue, purple), *Clematis* (red, purple, blue, white, pink), *Clethra* (white, pink), *Coreopsis* (yellow, pink), *Delphinium* (blue, pink, purple, white), *Digitalis* (pink, white, yellow), *Echinacea* (pink, white), *Echinops* (blue), *Gaura* (pink, white), *Geranium* (blue, purple, pink, white), *Hemerocallis* (yellow, orange, red, pink), *Heuchera* (pink, purple, white), *Hibiscus* (white, pink, purple, red, blue), *Hydrangea* (white, pink, blue), *Hypericum* (yellow, orange), *Iris* (purple, blue, white, yellow), *Lavandula* (purple, pink), *Leucanthemum* (white), *Liatris* (purple, white), *Lilium* (white, pink, red, yellow, orange), *Lupinus* (white, red, pink, yellow, blue, purple), *Monarda* (red, pink), *Nepeta* (blue, purple), *Paeonia* (pink, white, red, purple, yellow), *Perovskia* (blue, purple), *Phlox paniculata* (white, pink, purple, red), *Potentilla* (yellow), *Rosa* (white, yellow, red, pink, purple), *Rudbeckia* (yellow, orange), *Salvia* (blue, purple, white), *Spiraea* (white, pink), *Stewartia* (white)

## AUGUST

*Achillea* (yellow, orange, pink, white), *Alcea* (red, pink, purple, white, yellow), *Astilbe* (red, pink, white, purple), *Buddleia* (white, pink, purple, blue), *Calluna* (red, pink, purple, white), *Campanula* (blue, purple, white), *Campsis* (red), *Caryopteris* (blue, purple), *Clethra* (white, pink), *Coreopsis* (yellow, pink), *Echinacea* (pink, white), *Echinops* (blue), *Gaura* (pink, white), *Geranium* (blue, purple, pink, white), *Hemerocallis* (yellow, orange, red, pink), *Heptacodium* (white), *Hibiscus* (white, pink, purple, red, blue), *Hydrangea* (white, pink, blue), *Hypericum* (yellow, orange), *Lavandula* (purple, pink), *Leucanthemum* (white), *Liatris* (purple, white), *Lilium* (white, pink, red, yellow, orange), *Monarda* (red, pink), *Perovskia* (blue, purple), *Phlox paniculata* (white, pink, purple, red), *Potentilla* (yellow), *Rosa* (white, yellow, red, pink, purple), *Rudbeckia* (yellow, orange), *Sedum* (red, yellow, pink), *Spiraea* (white, pink)

## SEPTEMBER

*Achillea* (yellow, orange, pink, white), *Aconitum* (blue, purple), *Aster* (blue, purple, white, pink), *Buddleia* (white, pink, purple, blue), *Calluna* (red, pink, purple, white), *Caryopteris* (blue, purple), *Coreopsis* (yellow, pink), *Geranium* (blue, purple, pink, white), *Hydrangea* (white, pink, blue), *Lavandula* (purple, pink), *Monarda* (red, pink), *Potentilla* (yellow), *Rosa* (white, yellow, red, pink, purple), *Sedum* (red, yellow, pink)

## OCTOBER

*Aster* (blue, purple, white, pink), *Hamamelis*

(yellow, red), *Potentilla* (yellow), *Rosa* (white, yellow, red, pink, purple)

## NOVEMBER–DECEMBER

*Sarcococca* (white), *Viola* (purple, white, blue)

## JANUARY–FEBRUARY

*Erica carnea* 'Winter Beauty' (pink), *Hamamelis* (yellow, red), *Helleborus* (white, pink, purple), *Rhododendron mucronulatum* (purple), *Sarcococca* (white)

# PLANTS FOR COLORFUL FRUIT

*Amelanchier canadensis* (serviceberry): zone 3, dark blue, edible, July, 15–25' ht. deciduous tree, sun to part shade

*Callicarpa japonica* (Japanese beautyberry): zone 5, lilac, Oct–Nov, 4–6' ht. deciduous shrub, sun to part shade

*Cornus canadensis* (bunchberry): zone 3, red, August, 6–9" ht. deciduous groundcover, shade

*Cornus racemosa* (gray dogwood): zone 4, white, August, 10–15' ht. deciduous shrub, sun to shade

*Hypericum androsaemum* 'Albury Purple' (St. John's wort): zone 5, red, September, 2–4' ht. deciduous shrub, sun to part shade

*Ilex glabra* (inkberry): zone 5, blue-black, Sept, 3–6' ht. evergreen shrub, sun to shade

*Ilex* x *meserveae* 'Blue Princess' (Blue Princess holly): zone 5, red, Sept, 6–10' ht. evergreen shrub, sun to shade

*Ilex verticillata* (winterberry): zone 3, red, Sept, 6–10' ht. deciduous shrub, sun to part shade

*Mahonia aquifolium* (Oregon grape holly): zone 5, blue, Aug, 3–6' ht. evergreen shrub, shade

*Malus* sp. (flowering crabapple): zone 4, red-orange-yellow, Sept, 8–30' ht. deciduous tree, full sun

*Parthenocissus quinquefolia* (Virginia creeper): zone 4, blue, Sept–Oct, 30–50' ht. deciduous vine, sun to shade

*Rosa* sp. (rose): variable zones, red, July–Aug, 2–6' ht. deciduous shrub, full sun

*Symphoricarpos albus* (snowberry): zone 3, white, Sept, 3–6' ht. deciduous shrub, sun to shade

*Vaccinium corymbosum* (highbush blueberry): zone 3, dark blue, July–Aug, edible, 4–8' ht. deciduous shrub, sun to part shade

*Viburnum* sp. (viburnum): zone 2–5, dark blue, red, white, Sept–Oct, 5–12' ht. deciduous shrub, sun to part shade

# PLANTS FOR BARK

*Acer griseum* (paperbark maple): zone 5, cinnamon exfoliating bark, 20–30' ht deciduous tree, full sun

*Acer pensylvanicum* (striped maple): zone 3, green bark with white stripes, 15–20' ht. deciduous tree, part shade

*Amelanchier canadensis* (serviceberry): zone 3, light gray, smooth bark, 15–25' ht. deciduous tree, sun to part shade

*Betula alleghaniensis* (yellow birch): zone 3, gold exfoliating bark, 60–75' ht. deciduous tree, part shade

*Betula nigra* (river birch): zone 5, reddish brown to creamy exfoliating bark, 50–70' ht. deciduous tree, full sun

*Betula papyrifera* (paper birch): zone 2, white bark, 50–60' ht. deciduous tree, full sun

*Carpinus betulus* (hornbeam): zone 5, dark gray, smooth bark, 40–60' ht. deciduous tree, sun to part shade

*Cornus sericea* (redosier dogwood): zone 2, red bark, 6–10' ht. deciduous shrub, sun to part shade

*Cornus sericea* 'Flaviramea' (yellow twig dogwood): zone 2, yellow bark, 6–10' ht. deciduous shrub, sun to part shade

*Heptacodium miconioides* (seven son flower): zone 5, tan exfoliating bark, 15–20' ht. deciduous tree, full sun

*Hydrangea quercifolia* (oakleaf hydrangea): zone 5, cinnamon exfoliating bark, 6–10' h. deciduous shrub, sun to part shade

*Maackia amurensis* (amur maackia): zone 5, copper exfoliating bark, 20–30' ht. deciduous tree, full sun

*Phellodendron amurense* (amur corktree): zone 3, corky gray bark, 30–45' ht. deciduous tree, full sun

*Platanus x acerifolia* (London planetree): zone 5, patches of cream, green and tan bark, 40–50' ht. deciduous tree, sun to part shade

*Populus tremuloides* (quaking aspen): zone 1, gray-green bark, 40–50' ht. deciduous tree, sun to part shade

*Prunus maackii* (amur chokecherry): zone 2, bright yellow-orange bark, 35–45' ht. deciduous tree, full sun

*Prunus sargentii* (sargent cherry): zone 4, reddish bark, 40–50' ht. deciduous tree, full sun

*Prunus serrulata* (flowering cherry): zone 5, shiny red-brown bark, 20–25' ht. deciduous tree, full sun

*Salix alba* 'Tristis' (golden weeping willow): zone 2, yellowish-brown bark, 30–40' ht. deciduous tree, full sun

*Stewartia pseudocamellia* (Japanese stewartia): zone 6, patches of orange, gray and green bark, 20-40' ht. deciduous tree, full sun

*Ulmus parvifolia* (Chinese elm): zone 5, gray-green, exfoliating bark, 40–50' ht. deciduous tree, full sun

## PLANTS TO ATTRACT WILDLIFE (PRIMARILY BIRDS AND BUTTERFLIES)

*Amelanchier canadensis* (serviceberry): zone 3, 15–25' ht. deciduous tree, sun to part shade

*Aquilegia* sp. (columbine): zone 3, 10–30" ht. perennial, part shade

*Asclepias tuberosa* (butterfly weed): zone 4, 18–36" ht. perennial, full sun

*Buddleia davidii* (butterfly bush): zone 5, 3–5' ht. deciduous shrub, full sun

*Campsis radicans* (trumpet vine): zone 4, 30–40' ht. vine, full sun

*Chaenomeles speciosa* (flowering quince): zone 4, 3–10' ht. deciduous shrub, sun to part shade

*Clethra alnifolia* (summersweet): zone 3, 2–8' ht. deciduous shrub, sun to shade

*Cornus florida* (flowering dogwood): zone 4, 20–25' ht. deciduous tree, sun to part shade

*Cornus sericea* (redosier dogwood): zone 3, 6–10' ht. deciduous shrub, sun to shade

*Digitalis purpurea* (foxglove): zone 4, 24–48" ht. perennial, sun to part shade

*Echinacea purpurea* (coneflower): zone 3, 18–36" ht. perennial, full sun

*Hibiscus syriacus* (rose of Sharon): zone 5, 8–10' ht. deciduous shrub, sun to part shade

*Lobelia cardinalis* (cardinal flower): zone 3, 30–48" ht. perennial, sun to part shade

*Malus* sp. (flowering crabapple): zone 4, 8–30' ht. deciduous tree, full sun

*Monarda didyma* (beebalm): zone 4, 12–48" ht. perennial, sun to part shade

*Nepeta* x *faassenii* (catmint): zone 3, 12–36" ht. perennial, full sun

*Rhododendron* sp. (rhododendron): zone 4, 3–8' ht. evergreen shrub, part shade

*Rosa* sp. (rose): variable zones, 2–6' ht. deciduous shrub, full sun

*Vaccinium corymbosum* (highbush blueberry): zone 3, 4–8' ht. deciduous shrub, sun to part shade

*Viburnum* sp. (viburnum): zone 2–5, 5–12' ht. deciduous shrub, sun to part shade

*Weigela florida* (weigela): zone 5, 4–8' ht. deciduous shrub, full sun

# PLANTS FOR SPECIFIC ENVIRONMENTAL CONDITIONS

## WET SOILS

*Acer rubrum* (red maple)

*Amelanchier canadensis* (serviceberry)

*Andromeda polifolia* (bog rosemary)

*Azalea vaseyi* (pinkshell azalea)

*Azalea viscosum* (swamp azalea)

*Betula nigra* (river birch)

*Calycanthus floridus* (Carolina allspice)

*Clethra alnifolia* (summersweet)

*Cornus sericea* (redosier dogwood)

*Fraxinus pennsylvanica* (green ash)

*Gleditsia triacanthos* (honeylocust)

*Ilex glabra* (inkberry)

*Ilex verticillata* (winterberry)

*Itea virginica* (Virginia sweetspire)

*Lindera benzoin* (spicebush)

*Liquidambar styraciflua* (sweetgum)

*Magnolia virginiana* (sweetbay magnolia)

*Metasequoia glyptostroboides* (dawn redwood)

*Nyssa sylvatica* (tupelo)

*Quercus palustris* (pin oak)

*Salix* sp. (willow)

*Thuja occidentalis* (arborvitae)

*Vaccinium corymbosum* (blueberry)

*Viburnum dentatum* (arrowwood viburnum)

*Viburnum trilobum* (American cranberrybush)

## DRY SOILS

*Abies concolor* (white fir)

*Acer campestre* (hedge maple)

*Betula* sp. (birch)

*Calluna vulgaris* (heather)

*Carpinus betulus* (European hornbeam)

*Caryopteris* x *clandonensis* (bluebeard)

*Chaenomeles speciosa* (flowering quince)

*Cotinus coggygria* (smoketree)

*Crataegus* sp. (hawthorn)

*Fraxinus pennsylvanica* (green ash)

*Gleditsia triacanthos* (honeylocust)

*Hibiscus syriacus* (rose of Sharon)

*Juniperus* sp. (juniper)

*Philadelphus* sp. (mockorange)

*Pinus* sp. (pine)

*Platanus* x *acerifolia* (planetree)

*Potentilla fruticosa* (potentilla)

*Prunus maritima* (beach plum ()

*Rosa rugosa* (rugosa rose)

*Yucca filamentosa* (yucca)


## SHADE

*Acer campestre* (hedge maple)

*Acer palmatum* (Japanese maple)

*Amelanchier* sp. (serviceberry)

*Azalea* sp. (azalea)

*Calycanthus floridus* (Carolina allspice)

*Carpinus* sp. (hornbeam)

*Cercis canadensis* (redbud)

*Clethra alnifolia* (summersweet)

*Cornus* sp. (dogwood)

*Enkianthus campanulatus* (redvein
  enkianthus)

*Fothergilla* sp. (fothergilla)

*Hamamelis* sp. (witchhazel)

*Hydrangea* sp. (hydrangea)

*Ilex* sp. (holly)

*Itea virginica* (Virginia sweetspire)

*Kalmia latifolia* (mountain laurel)

*Kerria japonica* (Japanese kerria)

*Leucothoe* sp. (leucothoe)

*Ligustrum* sp. (privet)

*Lindera benzoin* (spicebush)

*Mahonia aquifolium* (Oregon grape holly)

*Oxydendron arboreum* (sourwood)

*Parthenocissus quinquefolia* (Virginia
  creeper)

*Pieris* sp. (andromeda)

*Rhododendron* sp. (rhododendron)

*Stephanandra incisa* (cutleaf stephanandra)

*Taxus* sp. (yew)

*Tsuga canadensis* (hemlock)

*Viburnum* sp. (viburnum)


## SEA COAST (WINDY, DRY, SUNNY)

*Acer ginnala* (amur maple)

*Aesculus hippocastanum* (horsechestnut)

*Buddleia davidii* (butterfly bush)

*Calluna vulgaris* (heather)

*Caryopteris* x clandonensis (blue mist spirea)

*Chamaecyparis pisifera* (falsecypress)

*Crataegus crusgalli* (cockspur hawthorn)

*Erica carnea* (heath)

*Fraxinus pennsylvanica* (green ash)

*Gleditsia triacanthos* (honeylocust)

*Hibiscus syriacus* (rose of Sharon)

*Ilex glabra* (inkberry)

*Juniperus* sp. (juniper)

*Lavendula* sp. (lavender)

*Lonicera tatarica* (tatarian honeysuckle)

*Picea pungens* (Colorado spruce)
*Pinus mugo* (mugo pine)
*Pinus nigra* (Austrian pine)
*Pinus sylvestris* (Scotch pine)
*Platanus* x *acerifolia* (London planetree)
*Potentilla fruticosa* (potentilla)
*Prunus maritima* (beach plum)
*Rosa rugosa* (rugosa rose)

# REFERENCES & SUGGESTED READING

American Nursery and Landscape Association (2004). *American Standard for Nursery Stock*. Washington, DC: American Nursery and Landscape Association.

Anella, Louis, Thomas C. Hennessey, and Edward M. Lorenzi (2008). "Growth of Balled-and-Burlapped versus Bare-Root Trees in Oklahoma, US." *Arboriculture & Urban Forestry* 34(3): 200–203.

Ausubel, Kenny, and J. P. Harpignies, Eds. (2004). *Nature's Operating Instructions: The True Biotechnologies*. San Francisco, CA: Sierra Club Books.

Bahamon, Alejandro, Patricia Perez, and Alex Campello (2006). *Inspired by Nature: Plants*. New York, NY: W. W. Norton & Company.

Bassuk, Nina, Jason Grabosky, and Peter Trowbridge (2005). *Using CU-Structural Soil™ in the Urban Environment*. Ithaca, NY: Cornell University Urban Horticulture Institute.

Benyus, Janine M. (1997). *Biomimicry: Innovation Inspired by Nature*. New York, NY: William Morrow.

Birren, Faber (1978). *Color & Human Response*. New York, NY: John Wiley & Sons.

Booth, Norman K. (1983). *Basic Elements of Landscape Architectural Design*. Prospect Heights, IL: Waveland Press.

Brady, Nyle C. (1990). *The Nature and Properties of Soils, 10th edition*. New York, NY: Macmillan.

Brickell, Christopher, and David Joyce (1996). *The American Horticultural Society: Pruning & Training*. New York, NY: DK Publishing.

Brownell, Blaine (2006). *Transmaterial: A Catalog of Materials That Redefine Our Physical Environment*. New York, NY: Princeton Architectural Press.

Brownell, Blaine (2008). *Transmaterial 2: A Catalog of Materials That Redefine Our Physical Environment*. New York, NY: Princeton Architectural Press.

Calkins, Meg (2009). *Materials for Sustainable Sites*. Hoboken, NJ: John Wiley & Sons.

Capon, Brian (2005). *Botany for Gardeners*. Portland, OR: Timber Press.

Carpenter, Philip L., Theodore D. Walker, and Frederick O. Lanphear (1975). *Plants in the Landscape*. San Francisco, CA: W. H. Freeman.

Chamberlin, Susan (1983). *Hedges, Screens, and Espaliers*. Tucson, AZ: HP Books.

Chaney, William R. (2002). *Does Night Lighting Harm Trees?* West Lafayette, IN: Purdue University Cooperative Extension (article FNR-FAQ-17).

De La Croix, Horst, Richard G. Tansey, and Diane Kirkpatrick (1991). *Art Through the Ages, 9th edition.* Fort Worth, TX: Harcourt Brace Jovanovich College Publishers.

Dirr, Michael A. (1998). *Manual of Woody Landscape Plants, 5th edition.* Champaign, IL: Stipes Publishing.

Dunnett, Nigel, and Noel Kingsbury (2008). *Planting Green Roofs & Living Walls.* Portland, OR: Timber Press.

Elam, Kimberly (2001). *Geometry of Design: Studies in Proportion and Composition.* New York, NY: Princeton Architectural Press.

Glattstein, Judy (2003). *Consider the Leaf: Foliage in Garden Design.* Portland, OR: Timber Press.

Graham, Linda E., James M. Graham, and Lee W. Wilcox (2006). *Plant Biology, 2nd edition.* Upper Saddle River, NJ: Pearson Education.

Hicks, Ivan, and Richard Rosenfeld (2007). *Tricks with Trees.* London: Pavilion Books.

Hobhouse, Penelope (1985). *Color in Your Garden.* London, UK: Frances Lincoln.

Humphrey, Dana N., and Michael Swett (2006). *Literature Review of the Water Quality Effects of Tire Derived Aggregate and Rubber Modified Asphalt Pavement.* Orono, ME: University of Maine Department of Civil and Environmental Engineering.

Jekyll, Gertrude (1983). *Colour Schemes for the Flower Garden.* Salem, NH: Ayer.

Jones, Owen (2001). *The Grammar of Ornament.* Paris, France: L'Aventurine.

Kaplan, Rachel, Stephen Kaplan, and Robert L. Ryan (1998). *With People in Mind.* Washington, DC: Island Press.

Krussmann, Gerd (2002). *Pocket Guide to Choosing Woody Ornamentals.* Portland, OR: Timber Press.

Lawson, Andrew (1996). *The Gardener's Book of Color: Creating Contrasts, Harmonies, and Multi-colored Themes in Your Garden.* Pleasantville, NY: Reader's Digest Association.

Mahnke, Frank H (1996). *Color, Environment, and Human Response.* New York, NY: John Wiley & Sons.

McDonough, William, and Michael Braungart (2002). *Cradle to Cradle: Remaking the Way We Make Things.* New York, NY: North Point Press.

Neely, Dan, and Gary W. Watson, Eds. (1998). *The Landscape Below Ground II: Proceedings of an International Workshop on Tree Root Development in Urban Soils.* Champaign, IL: International Society of Arboriculture.

Papanek, Victor (1971). *Design for the Real World: Human Ecology and Social Change.* New York, NY: Pantheon.

Posamentier, Alfred S., and Ingmar Lehmann. *The (Fabulous) Fibonacci Numbers* (2007). Amherst, NY: Prometheus Books.

Rakow, Donald A., and Richard Weir III (1989). *Pruning: An Illustrated Guide to Pruning Ornamental Trees and Shrubs.* Ithaca, NY: Cornell Cooperative Extension.

Robinson, Nick (2004). *The Planting Design Handbook, 2nd edition.* Aldershot, UK: Ashgate Publishing.

Shigo, Alex (1994). *Tree Anatomy.* Durham, NH: Shigo & Trees Associates.

Sovinski, Rob W. (2009). *Materials and Their Applications in Landscape Design.* Hoboken, NJ: John Wiley & Sons.

Still, Steven M. (1994). *Manual of Herbaceous Ornamental Plants, 4th edition.* Champaign, IL: Stipes Publishing.

Sullivan, Joseph P. (2006). *An Assessment of Environmental Toxicity and Potential Contamination from Artificial Turf Using Shredded or Crumb Rubber.* Woodland, CA: Ardea Consulting.

Turner, Kimberly D. (2001). "Childhood Memories of Landscapes as a Restorative Tool in Designing Outdoor Environments for Alzheimer Patients." Master's thesis, University of Massachusetts Amherst.

Van der Ryn, Sim, and Stewart Cowan (1996). *Ecological Design*. Washington, DC: Island Press.

Watson, Gary W., and Dan Neely, Eds. (1994). *The Landscape Below Ground: Proceedings of an International Workshop on Tree Root Development in Urban Soils*. Savoy, IL: International Society of Arboriculture.

Wilder, Louise Beebe. (1974). *The Fragrant Garden: A Book About Sweet Scented Flowers & Leaves*. New York, NY: Dover.

Wilhide, Elizabeth (2001). *Materials: A Directory for Home Design*. London, UK: Quadrille Publishing.

Yeang, Ken (1995). *Designing with Nature: The Ecological Basis for Architectural Design*. New York, NY: McGraw Hill.

# INDEX

expansive soil, 42
eye-level plants, 61

*Fagus*, 65, 141. *See also* beech
    *Fagus sylvatica* 'Pendula,' 92
Farrand, Beatrix, 90–91
fastigiate plants, 54, 55, 95, *95*
feeder roots, 121
fertilization, 41, 130–31, 134
Fescue 'Elijah Blue', 84, *84*
*Festuca glauca* 'Elijah Blue'. *See*
    Fescue 'Elijah Blue'
Fibonacci sequence, 104–5
filament, 70
fleshy fruits, 72, 73
Flexi-pave, 123
flowers, 68–71
    anatomy, 69–70, *70*
    arrangements, 71
    complete vs. incomplete, 70
    design features of, 68, *68*, 71
    monoecious vs. dioecious,
      70–71
    perfect vs. imperfect, 70
    prompts for, 37
    sexual reproduction, 70–71
flying buttresses, 167, *167*
follies, 140
forced perspective, 100
form, 53–56, 133–46
formal design, 102, *102*, 108–10,
    *108*, 140
forsythia, 135, 144
    *Forsythia*, 52, 63, 88, 136
fragrance, 75–76
*Fraxinus*, 52, 63. *See also* ash
French Provincial style, 109
fruit, 72–74
    biological function, 72
    maintenance, 73–74
    poisonous, 74
    ripening, 32
    types, 72–73
fruit trees, 143
fuchsia, 170

full shade, 39
full sun, 39
functional roles of plants, 93–102
    architecture, as complement
      to, 93–96
    privacy and safety, 96–98
    scale, 96
    views, 92, 98–99
    visual manipulation of space,
      92, 99–102

gardener–landscape designer
    relationship, 126–27, 132
*Gaura lindheimeri*, 109
genetic engineering, 25
genetics
    in design, 25–26
    in nature, 23–25
genus, 18, 19
geometric design, 102, 140, 142,
    *143*
*Geranium*, 128
    *Geranium* 'Blue Blood,' 92
    *Geranium* 'Johnson's Blue,' 90
    *Geranium* sp., 60
*Geum*, 88
gibberellins, 32
*Ginkgo biloba* 'Princeton Sentry,'
    95
ginkgo trees, 73, *73*
girdling roots, 113, 122
*Gleditsia triacanthos*, 49, 63–64
    *Gleditsia triacanthos*
      'Shademaster,' 98
golden ratio, 103–7
Gothic Revival style, 95
Gothic style, 166
grafting, 145–46
grass
    mown, 60
    ornamental, 54, *54*
gravitropism, 31–32
gray, 81
Greece, 165
green, 86–87

green design, 155–71
    biomimicry, 165–69
    closed water systems, 164
    environmental improvement/
      enhancement, 156–61
    evolution, 169–71
    green roofs, 161–62
    LEED certification, 155–56
    materials selection, 164–65
    vertical gardens, 163–64
Green Planet Paints, 169
green roofs, 161–62, *161*, *162*
ground-level plants, 60–61, *60*
groundcovers, 60
grouping, 107
growth. *See also* aging landscape
    design decisions based on, 52,
      57–59, *58*
    hormones affecting, 31–32
    synthetic hormones for,
      32–33
    temperature and, 34
growth regulators, 32–33
gymnosperms, 69, 74, 149

habits, 52–62
    form, 53–56
    size, 57–62
    texture, 56–57
*Hakonechloa macra* 'Aureola,' 80,
    83
hardiness zones, 34–36, *35*, 49
hardscape, 147
hardwood, 148–49
Harry Lauder's walking stick, 55
head (flower), 71
heading back, 139
health evaluation, 113–16
heart pine, 152–53
heartwood, 147–48
heat reflection, 37, 49, 157
heat zones, 36, *36*
heavy metals, 44
*Hedera*, 74
    *Hedera helix*, 60, 120

lotus leaf, 168
lumber. *See* wood

macronutrients, 41
magnesium, 41
*Magnolia*, 92
    *Magnolia* x *loebneri*, 20, *20*
magnolias, 57
x *Mahoberberis*, 20
mahogany, 149, 151–52, *152*, *153*
*Mahonia*, 57
main leader, 135, 137, 139
maintenance, 126–31
    cones, 74
    deadheading, 128
    disease-fighting, 47, 129
    dividing, 128
    fertilization, 130–31
    formal gardens, 102
    fruits, 73–74
    insect prevention, 129
    irrigation, 127–28
    lawn care, 130
    mechanical damage
        prevention, 50
    mulch, 129
    necessity of, 127
    pest-fighting, 47, 129
    pruning and thinning, 58,
        129, 133–40
    soil, 127
    vertical gardens, 164
    weeding, 128
    winter damage and snow
        removal, 129–30
*Malus* 'Prairiefire,' 74
maple, *67*, 152, *153*. *See also* Acer
marigolds, 105
'Matsu' apple trees, *114*
maturity. *See* aging landscape
mechanical damage, 49–50
memory, 75
Mendel, Gregor, 24
Michelangelo Buonarroti, 103
microclimates

defined, 36–37
plant selection, 33, 36–37
shaping of plant forms, 32
soil selection, 46
urban, 47
windy, 49
micronutrients, 41, 131
*Miscanthus sinensis*, 61. *See also*
    ornamental grasses
mockorange, 95
modification. *See* physical
    modification
*Monarda*, 88
    *Monarda didyma* 'Jacob
        Cline,' 83
monoecious flowers, 70
morphology, 51–76
    bark, 74–75
    flowers, 68–71
    form, 53–56
    fragrance, 75–76
    fruit, 72–74
    habits, 52–62
    leaves, 62–68
    size, 57–62
    texture, 56–57
mountain laurel, 69, *69*. *See also*
    Kalmia
mowing, 130
mown grass, 60
mulch, 119, 124–25, *124*, 129
multiple fruits, 73
multistemmed trees, 56, *56*
mutations, 24
mutualistic symbiosis, 170
mycorrhizae, 119, 170
*Myosotis*, 84

*Narcissus*, 92
native soil, 119
native species, 165
natural selection, 24–25. *See also*
    evolution
naturalistic plantings, 21, *22*, 108
Neoclassicism, *94*

*Nepeta*, 90
nitrogen, 41, 131
nodes, 63
noise abatement, 159
nomenclature, 18–19
Norway spruce, 108. *See also* Picea
nucleus, 29
nurseries, 22–23, 173–74
nutrients, 30–31, 41, 130–31

oak, 73, 149, 152. *See also* Quercus
oakleaf hydrangea, 65. *See also*
    Hydrangea
Olmsted, Frederick Law, 160, 167
orchids, 170, *170*
organic matter, 42, 127, 131
ornamental grasses, 54, *54*, 109
osmosis, 28–29
oval plants, 54
ovary, 70
ovules, 69, 70

*Pachysandra*, 125
*Paeonia*, 81, 128
    *Paeonia* 'Monsieur Jules Elie,'
        85
    *Paeonia* 'Tom Eckhardt,' 85
paint
    eco-friendly, 169
    pruning wound treatment,
        138
    water-repellent paint, 168–69
palm trees, 94
palmately compound leaf, 64, *64*
*Papaver*, 71. *See also* poppies
    *Papaver orientale* 'King
        Kong,' 86
paperbark maple, 75. *See also* Acer,
    A. griseum
parasitic symbiosis, 170
parterre gardens, 101–2
pastoralism, 160
pathways, 100, *101*. *See also* desire
    lines; pedestrian traffic